modern
STYLE for Girls

Sew a Boutique Wardrobe

Mary Abreu

stash BOOKS.

an imprint of C&T Publishing

Text copyright © 2015 by Mary Abreu

Photography and artwork copyright © 2015 by C&T Publishing, Inc.

Publisher: Amy Marson

Creative Director: Gailen Runge

Art Director: Kristy Zacharias

Editor: Liz Aneloski

Technical Editors: Helen Frost and Alison M. Schmidt

Cover Designers: Kristy Zacharias and April Mostek

Book Designer: Katie McIntosh

Page Layout Artist: April Mostek

Production Coordinators/Illustrators: Jenny Davis and Zinnia Heinzmann

Production Editor: Alice Mace Nakanishi

Photo Assistant: Mary Peyton Peppo

Style photography by Mary Abreu and instructional photography by Diane Pedersen, unless otherwise noted

Published by Stash Books, an imprint of C&T Publishing, Inc., P.O. Box 1456, Lafayette, CA 94549

Library of Congress Cataloging-in-Publication Data

Abreu, Mary.

  Modern style for girls : sew a boutique wardrobe / Mary Abreu.

    pages cm

  ISBN 978-1-61745-081-5 (soft cover)

  1. Girls' clothing. 2. Dressmaking--Patterns. I. Title.

  TT562.A274 2015

  646.4'04--dc23

                          2015008229

Printed in China

10 9 8 7 6 5 4 3 2 1

4/2016

DEDICATION

For my folks, Jo Lambert and John Abreu. I couldn't ask for more supportive and encouraging parents. I love you!

ACKNOWLEDGMENTS

I couldn't do this without my amazing husband, Matt. YMEAMB.

Lisa Carroccio (a.k.a. The Diva™) is the first person I turn to for guidance. I'm so fortunate to have her in my corner.

This book might not have happened without the regular encouragement (and prodding) of Sarah Phillips. My life would also be lacking funky shoes, shopping trips, WaHo, and ridiculous donuts were she not in it.

Thank you to my awesome pattern testers: Cheryl Arkison, MaryAnn Lopes, and Hayden Thornton. Y'all rock!

Caden Kluge jumped in and helped knock out how-to models, iron fabric, organize samples, and make sure I took regular breaks from the sewing machine to do little things, like eat. She's pretty awesome!

Dana Konick and Amor Owens—thanks for making my other career dream a reality!

I just love these gals: Amanda Wood, Amber Hartenbower, Bari Ackerman, Jona Giammalva, Tifani Keith, Kristina Milling, Meredith Placko, and Veda Behfarshad.

The beautiful little girls wearing these clothes hold a special place in my heart. Thank you Shaudi, Kayla, Jadyn, and especially Liesl.

Thank you, Andover Fabrics, Michael Miller Fabrics, Dear Stella, FreeSpirit Fabrics, and Intown Quilters, for providing many of the fabrics used throughout this book.

Liz Aneloski, you rock! And big thanks to all the C&T folks who helped this book go from concept to paper.

Many, many thanks to the thousands of people around the world who have made my first book—*Little Girls, Big Style*—a part of their sewing libraries. It warms my heart to see your emails, pictures, blog posts, and social media comments.

Contents

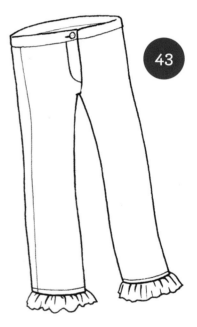

Preface

School picture day, 2011:

My lovely daughter was in second grade. I spent the hours after she went to bed sewing a Knotty Apron Dress for her to wear the next morning for school pictures. I changed the ruffle at the hem to a hem band, per her request, but added a tiny bit of ruching on the bodice.

"Do you have to put ruffles on everything?" she asked with a disappointed sigh.

Ouch.

Gone were the days of making clothes for my child without her input—at least if I wanted her to actually wear them. My mom friends and I commiserated about the challenges of outfitting our girls, who suddenly decided they were too old for ruffle pants and big hair bows, yet too young to wear scaled-down teen fashions.

But then an interesting thing happened. I involved my daughter in choosing clothing patterns and fabric, letting her style shine through. I modified patterns to make them more age appropriate and curbed my desire to throw on more ruffles. (Ruffle all the things!)

It wasn't long before she not only outgrew the patterns from *Little Girls, Big Style* but also inspired an all-new set of wardrobe options for me to create—and then share with you.

These days, she'll excitedly bring me her sketchbook—complete with fabric swatches—to show off her outfit ideas. And I know it won't be long before she'll bypass me and sew her own wardrobe. Until then, I'll happily work with her to bring those sketches to life.

Get the Look

Modified Lace-Trimmed Shorts (page 38) and Layers of Love Skirt (page 66)

HOW TO USE THIS BOOK

The projects in this book are divided into three sections: Basic Bodice, Pants, and Skirts. These projects can be created in girls' sizes 7–12. The handy sizing chart below should help you select the perfect size to sew.

Size	Chest	Waist	Hip
7	26″	23″	27″
8	27″	23½″	28″
9	27¾″	24″	29″
10	28½″	24½″	29½″
12	30″	25½″	31½″

Projects are sewn from a mix of pattern pieces and basic rectangles. Be sure to read the cutting instructions and pattern preparations carefully before you begin to cut your fabric. Most yardage requirements are based on the largest size, so you may have some extra fabric if you are making the smaller sizes. Fabric requirements and cutting layouts work for all fabrics, including those with a directional print or nap. If using a nondirectional fabric, you may be able to modify the cutting layout and use less fabric.

Modified Collared A-Line Dress (page 17)

I always recommend that my sewing students make a muslin (sometimes called a *toile*) when using a pattern for the first time. There's nothing more heartbreaking than spending hours creating a garment, only to find it doesn't fit—especially when you use treasured fabric. I tend to purchase clearance fabric for $1–$3 per yard for these test garments.

Use the patterns (pullout pages P1 and P2). All seam allowances are included. So, just select the size you need; check the project for what pattern pieces are needed; and trace the patterns onto a pattern paper, such as Pattern-Ease (by HTC Retail, Inc.) or Swedish tracing paper, following the instructions in Tracing Patterns (page 86).

All projects in the book refer to Techniques A–Z (page 75) for commonly used skills such as gathering, creating waistband casings, hemming, finishing seam allowances, and adding zipper insertions.

The sewing techniques in this book are a step up from those in my first book, *Little Girls, Big Style* (also by Stash Books). While the skirts still have elastic waistbands, the pants all have set-on waistbands, adjustable elastic in the back of the waist, and a zipper fly. You'll also learn to insert an invisible zipper!

The pattern "hacks" (modifications) have grown a little more complex in the Basic Bodice section (page 11). Project instructions walk you through converting a simple bodice pattern to a wrap-style top/dress, an A-line minidress with Peter Pan collar, and a pullover tunic.

CHOOSING FABRIC

Many projects in this book use premium quilting cotton for tops, dresses, and skirts, along with some voiles and lawns. While you certainly can use quilting cotton for shorts and pants, I prefer to sew with a bottom-weight fabric, such as corduroy or denim. The fabric is a slightly heavier weight and better suited for pants and zippers, in my opinion.

Selecting fabrics for a project is one of my favorite activities, especially when my daughter is involved. Tweens often have a definite idea of what they will and won't wear when it comes to color, print, and even texture. While my preschooler wouldn't hesitate to wear loud, clashing prints with acres of ruffles, my fourth-grader prefers solids and subtler prints. My younger sewing students echo those preferences, relegating anything resembling a novelty print to pajama pants and quirky accessories.

For me, the process starts with choosing the clothing patterns. Unless I'm sewing a skirt or a dress, I always plan an entire outfit before we pick the fabric, even if it includes something we're going to buy, such as a blouse or leggings.

I break down the garment by the number of fabrics that I plan to use. For example, this version of Modern Tunic (at right) uses two fabrics—one fabric for the tunic, another for the hem bands—while the Cuffed Dig 'Ems use two fabrics (though they could use just one). To tie it all together, I opted to make the pant cuffs from the same fabric that I used for the hem bands on the tunic.

So many people get overwhelmed by choosing fabric. Believe me, I feel your pain! I rarely pick out fabric for my daughter's clothes without her input, since we have vastly different tastes. She really likes pairing a single print, such as a floral, with either a solid or a low-key fabric, such as a polka dot or a tone-on-tone print (what quilters refer to as *blenders*).

Most fabric manufactured for the home-sewing market is produced in collections: coordinating fabrics meant to work together. Fabric designers typically mix up the scale of prints—large, medium, and small—to add variety that appeals to quilters and garment sewers alike. The explosive demand for solid fabrics and apparel-weight fabrics makes it even easier to find fabric for making garments.

But why limit yourself to a single collection when planning an outfit? I often see beautiful clothes made with a mix of florals and prints that leave me wondering, *Why didn't I think of that?!* The key is to find fabrics that "play well together," usually because they share a palette or because the scales of the prints don't compete with each other.

Coordinating Modern Tunic (page 30) and Cuffed Dig 'Ems (page 52)

Fabrics: Lovelorn Collection by Jenean Morrison for FreeSpirit Fabrics

Speaking of scale… it's important to consider the size of prints when choosing your fabrics. While some large-scale prints can easily be cut down, most need more room to shine. Smaller prints often are the most versatile, as are solids.

EMBELLISHMENTS

Now that I'm sewing for a tween—and an opinionated one, at that—I've had to take a different approach to embellishments. No more adding ruffle after ruffle to everything I sew.

If your child is less ruffle averse, then go ahead and add them as you wish! I love a 4″ (finished) ruffle at the hem of the Sleeveless Empire-Waist Top/Dress (page 12) or a dainty 1″ ruffle framing the neckline of the Wrap Top/Dress (page 22).

Have you added a serger to your sewing room? I use mine to overlock all my seam allowances, but I also put it to use adding rolled hems (page 84) to many of the garments I sew. The serger offers such a fast, easy way to add a little flair and the perfect touch to the hem. Depending on the garment, I will trim the hem allowance to ¼″, or (more likely) I'll leave the full hem allowance intact, so the item has a little more growing room.

Ruching—a strip of fabric with finished edges gathered in the center—quickly dresses up the center of a bodice. Either finish the edges with a narrow hem or use your serger to add a rolled hem on both edges.

Bias tape, lace, ribbon, and rickrack are staples in many sewing rooms. They make great accents, either attached to the hem or sewn above the hem of a garment. A small amount of double-sided fusible web, such as Heat*n*Bond Lite or Stitch Witchery, can hold your embellishment in place as you sew it to your garment.

Embroidery—whether by hand or machine—and appliqué can add a personal element to any garment. I splurged on an embroidery machine a few years ago and love how easy it is to add a little something extra to a garment. A small design on pants pockets or around a collar is subtle, yet fun. Or consider something like a trailing swirl to stretch up a pants leg or an artsy, one-color, sketch-style piece for the bottom of a tunic. My personal favorite sources of machine and appliqué designs are urbanthreads.com, emblibrary.com, and swakembroidery.com.

Embroidery design: urbanthreads.com

Basic
BODICE

Sleeveless Empire-Waist Top/Dress

Fabric: Field Day collection by Josephine Kimberling for Blend Fabrics; chambray from Andover Fabrics

Whether it's a top or a dress, this empire-waist style is a great wardrobe building block. Make it super casual in a solid fabric or even a sweet polka dot. Dress it up in fancier fabrics such as silk or taffeta. It's easy to add sleeves for cooler weather, too. Give it the illusion of a sash by adding a contrast fabric to the bodice bottom.

MATERIALS

- ½ yard for Bodice
- ½ yard for Bodice Lining
- ⅞ yard for Skirt (top version)
- 1⅜ yards for Skirt (dress version)
- 14″ invisible zipper

CUTTING

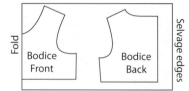

Cutting layout (use Bodice layout for Bodice Lining)

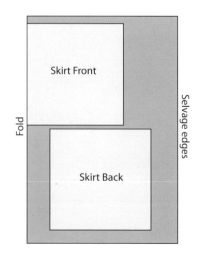

Bodice

Note: *Use Empire Top/Dress neckline and hemlines on Bodice Front and Bodice Back pattern pieces. Trim ¼″ from armscye on both pieces prior to cutting out your fabric.*

- Trace the appropriate size of the Bodice Front and Bodice Back patterns (pullout page P1) onto pattern paper (see Tracing Patterns, page 86).
- Cut 1 Bodice Front on the fold.
- Cut 2 Bodice Backs.

. . . .

Cutting continues

Skirt

All pieces are listed as length × width. For pieces cut on the fold, you need only half of the width measurement.

Cut	Size 7	Size 8	Size 9	Size 10	Size 12
Top Front (Cut 1.)	11¼″ × 26¾″	11¾″ × 27¼″	12¼″ × 27½″	12½″ × 28½″	13″ × 29¾″
Top Back (Cut 2.)	11¼″ × 14″	11¾″ × 14½″	12¼″ × 15″	12½″ × 15½″	13″ × 16″
Dress Front (Cut 1.)	21″ × 26¾″	21½″ × 27¼″	22″ × 27½″	22½″ × 28½″	23″ × 29¾″
Dress Back (Cut 2.)	21″ × 14″	21½″ × 14½″	22″ × 15″	22½″ × 15½″	23 × 16″

Bodice Lining

- Cut 1 Bodice Front on fold.
- Cut 2 Bodice Backs.

CONSTRUCTION

Seam allowances are ½″ unless otherwise noted.

1. Match the Bodice Front with the Bodice Back pieces at the shoulders, right sides together. Pin and sew. Press the seam allowances open.

2. Repeat Step 1 with the Bodice Lining pieces. Press the bottom edge of the Bodice Lining ½″ toward the wrong side of the fabric.

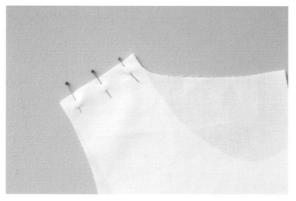

Match Bodice Front and Back at shoulder seams.

Press bottom edge of Bodice Lining ½″ toward wrong side of fabric.

3. Match the Bodice and Bodice Lining, right sides together. Pin at the neckline and armscye openings. Sew with a ¼″ seam allowance. Clip the seam allowances around the curves.

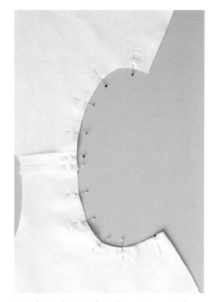

Match Bodice and Bodice Lining, right sides together. Pin and sew together at neckline and armscye.

4. Turn the Bodice right side out by pushing the Bodice Back pieces between the seams at the shoulders. Press the seams so the seam allowances are toward the Bodice Lining.

5. Understitch (page 87) the armscye openings and neckline. Press the Bodice flat.

6. With the fabrics right sides together, match the side seams of the Bodice and Bodice Linings. Pin and sew the side seams in one pass (one continuous line of stitching).

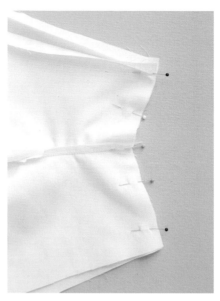

Match Bodice and Bodice Lining side seams.

7. Press the seam allowances open. Press the Bodice flat and set it aside.

8. Match the side seams of the Skirt Front panel with the Skirt Back panels. Pin and sew. Finish the seam allowances as desired (see Finishing Seams, page 77) and press.

Match Skirt pieces at side seams.

9. Sew gathering stitches to the top edge of the Skirt, using the method of your choice (see Gathering, page 77). Start and end your gathering stitches ½″ in from the center back opening of the Skirt.

10. Place the right side of the Skirt against the right side of the Bodice, matching the top edge of the Skirt to the bottom edge of the Bodice. Flip the Bodice Lining out of the way. Gather, pin, and sew the skirt to the Bodice only.

Gather Skirt to bottom edge of Bodice, but not to Bodice Lining.

11. Press the seam allowances toward the Bodice.

12. Topstitch (page 86) on the right side of the Bodice along the edge, slightly above the skirt. Take care to keep the Bodice Lining away from the stitching.

13. Insert an invisible zipper (page 91) in the center back seam.

14. Hem by pressing the bottom edge of the Skirt ¼″ toward the wrong side of the fabric and then again ½″. Stitch close to the upper folded edge to finish the hem.

15. Turn the Top/Dress inside out and slipstitch the Bodice Lining to the Bodice seam allowances.

Collared A-Line Dress

I am a huge fan of the TV show *Mad Men* and all things Wes Anderson, and this dress was definitely inspired by that retro vibe. My preference is to make the hem fall just above the knee, but obviously you can make it longer if you choose.

MATERIALS

- 2½ yards* for Dress
- ⅓ yard for Collar
- ⅓ yard midweight interfacing for Collar
- 14″ invisible zipper

* Yardage will vary based on length chosen.

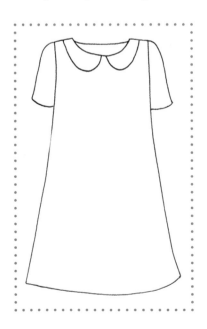

PREPARING THE PATTERN

1. Trace the appropriate size Bodice Front and Bodice Back patterns (pullout page P1) onto pattern paper (see Tracing Patterns, page 86), leaving enough room to extend the pattern in length and width.

2. Extend the center front line to the desired length and add an additional ½″ for the hem allowance.

3. Draw a line perpendicular to the center front line, extending approximately 5″ past the existing side seam.

4. Extend the side seam straight down to the perpendicular line from Step 3. Measure 3½″ beyond the side seam line and make a mark.

5. Place a ruler at the top of the side seam, extending down to the mark you just made; draw an angled line. This will be your new side seam.

6. Repeat Steps 2–5 with the Back Bodice piece. Before cutting, match the pattern pieces to make sure that your new side seams and hems align.

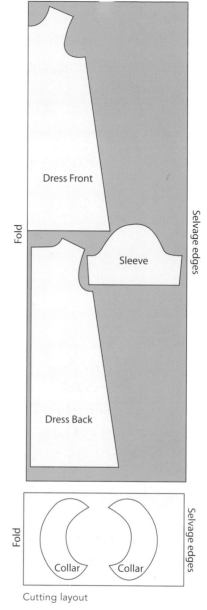

Cutting layout

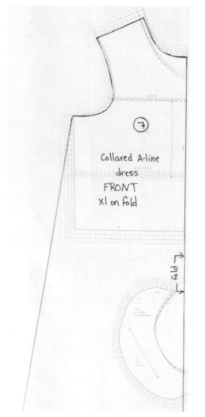

Modify Bodice Front pattern to make Dress Front.

Modify Bodice Back pattern to make Dress Back.

CUTTING

Bodice

- Cut 1 Dress Front on fold.
- Cut 2 Dress Backs.

Sleeves

- Cut 2 Sleeves.

Collar

- Cut 4 Collar pieces from fabric.
- Cut 2 Collar pieces from interfacing.

CONSTRUCTION

Seam allowances are ½" unless otherwise noted.

1. Match the Dress Front with the Dress Back at the shoulders, right sides together. Pin and sew. Finish the seam allowances as desired (see Finishing Seams, page 77) and press.

Match Dress Front with Dress Back at shoulder seams.

2. Follow the manufacturer's directions to fuse interfacing to one set of Collar fabric pieces.

3. Match an interfaced Collar piece with a noninterfaced Collar piece. Pin and sew with a ¼" seam allowance, sewing only the outer curved edge.

4. Clip the curves, turn right side out, and press well.

5. Repeat Steps 2–4 with the remaining Collar pieces.

6. Place the Collar on the neckline of the Dress, with the front edge of the Collar meeting at the center front of the Dress. Pin and sew using a ¼" seam allowance.

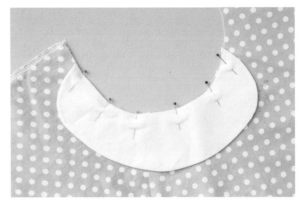

Match Collar to neckline of Dress.

7. Finish the raw edges of the neckline/collar as desired (see Finishing Edges, page 76). Press toward the wrong side of the dress.

8. Lift the Collar away from the Dress and understitch (page 87) through the Dress and the seam allowances.

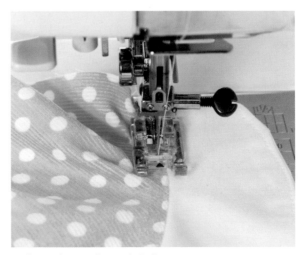

Understitch Dress beneath Collar seam.

9. Sew a row of ease stitching (see Ease Stitching, page 76) between the marks on the Sleeve cap.

Sew ease stitches on Sleeve cap.

10. Match the Sleeve and Dress armscye, right sides together. Pin and sew.

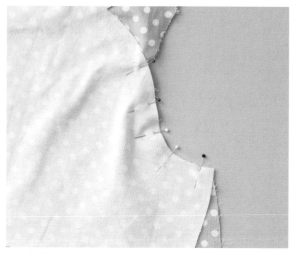

Match Sleeve to Dress armscye.

11. Finish the seam allowances as desired (see Finishing Seams, page 77). Press the seam toward the Dress.

12. Repeat Steps 9–11 with the second Sleeve.

13. With the fabrics right sides together, match the side seams of the Sleeve and Dress Front with the Dress Back. Sew the side seams together in one pass (a continuous line of stitching).

14. Finish the seam allowances as desired and press.

15. Insert an invisible zipper (page 91) in the center back of the Dress.

16. Hem the Sleeves by pressing ¼″ toward the wrong side of the fabric and then another ¼″. Stitch close to the inner folded edge.

17. Hem the Dress by pressing ¼″ toward the wrong side of the fabric and then another ¼″. Stitch close to the inner folded edge.

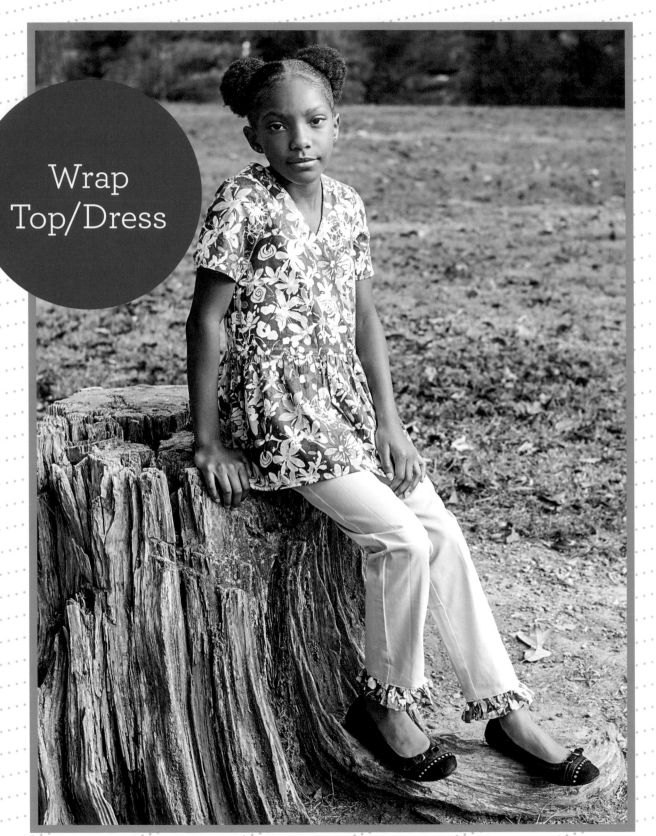

Wrap Top/Dress

Fabrics: Botanica by Felicity Miller for FreeSpirit Fabrics; cotton sateen by Michael Miller Fabrics

This Wrap Top/Dress is so versatile. It goes from casual to fancy with just a simple change of fabrics. And you can't beat a pattern that can be either a dress or a top! Slip it on like a robe, then fasten the crossover, fully-lined bodice with buttons. A second front skirt panel keeps her from worrying about peekaboo moments on the playground.

MATERIALS

- 1¾ yards for Top version
- 2½ yards for Dress version
- ⅔ yard for Bodice Lining
- 4 buttons (¾″)
- 1 two-piece snap (size 7)

PREPARING THE PATTERN

1. Trace the appropriate size Bodice Back pattern (pullout page P1) onto pattern paper (see Tracing Patterns, page 86), eliminating ½″ from the center back. Mark the new center back "Cut 1 on fold."

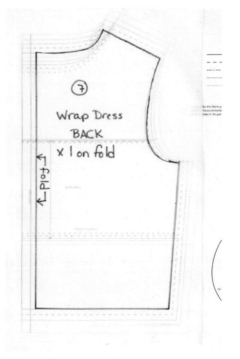

Remove ½″ from center back of Bodice Back to create new "cut on fold" line.

2. Trace the Bodice Front pattern (pullout page P1) onto pattern paper; flip the paper to trace the pattern piece again, creating a complete single-layer pattern for the Bodice Front.

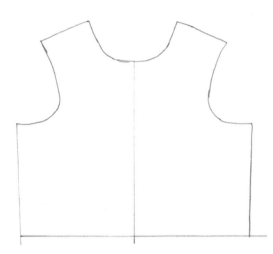

Trace Bodice Front pattern twice to create single, complete Bodice Front pattern piece to modify.

3. Measure 2½″ from the bottom of the neckline and mark this point on your pattern.

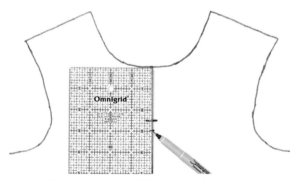

Measure from bottom of neckline and mark pattern.

4. Measure 1″ from the underarm on the right-hand side of the pattern (left Bodice Front) and mark your pattern.

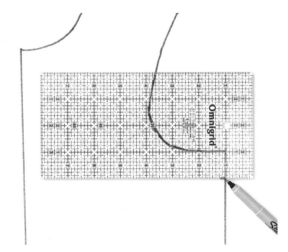

Mark 1″ from underarm of right-hand side of pattern.

5. Starting at the top left neckline, draw a gently curved line that passes through the first mark (neckline) and ends at the second mark (underarm).

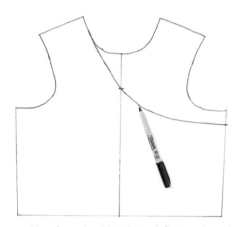

Draw curved line from shoulder, through first mark, and ending at second mark to create new neckline.

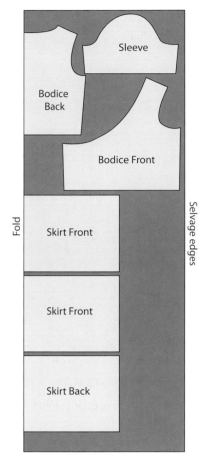

Cutting layout

CUTTING

Bodice

- Cut 1 Bodice Back on fold.
- Cut 2 Bodice Fronts.

Sleeves

- Cut 2 Sleeves.

Lining

- Cut 1 Bodice Back on fold.
- Cut 2 Bodice Fronts.

Skirt

All pieces are listed as length × width. For pieces cut on the fold, you need only half of the width measurement.

Cut	Size 7	Size 8	Size 9	Size 10	Size 12
Top Front (Cut 2.)	11½″ × 26¾″	12″ × 27″	12¼″ × 27½″	12½″ × 28″	13″ × 29½″
Top Back (Cut 1.)	11½″ × 26¾″	12″ × 27″	12¼″ × 27½″	12½″ × 28″	13″ × 29½″
Dress Front (Cut 2.)	23″ × 26¾″	23½″ × 27″	23¾″ × 27½″	24″ × 28″	24½″ × 29½″
Dress Back (Cut 1.)	23″ × 26¾″	23½″ × 27″	23¾″ × 27½″	24″ × 28″	24½″ × 29½″

CONSTRUCTION

Seam allowances are ½" unless otherwise noted.

1. Match the Bodice Fronts to the Bodice Backs at the shoulders, right sides together. Pin and sew. Press the seam allowances open.

2. Repeat Step 1 with the Lining Fronts and Lining Back.

3. Match the Bodice with the Lining, right sides together. Pin and sew along the neckline edge and the short edges at the front of the overlap.

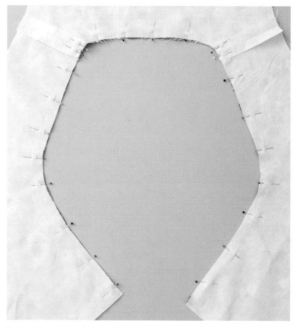

Pin and sew Bodice neckline and short edges at front of overlap.

4. Clip the curves of the seam allowances around the neckline.

5. Press the Lining over the seam allowances and understitch (page 87). Stitch through the Lining and seam allowance along the neckline only.

6. Press the Lining to the wrong side of the Bodice. Baste the Lining and the Bodice fabrics at the raw edges (armscye, side seams, and bottom edge). You will now treat the Bodice and Lining as one piece.

7. Sew a row of ease stitching (see Ease Stitching, page 76) between the marks on the Sleeve cap.

Sew ease stitches on Sleeve cap.

8. Match the Sleeve and Bodice armscye, right sides together. Pin and sew.

Match Sleeve to Bodice armscye.

9. Finish the seam allowances as desired (see Finishing Seams, page 77) and press toward the Bodice.

10. Repeat Steps 7–9 with the second Sleeve.

11. Match under the Sleeve seam and the side seams, right sides together. Pin and sew.

Match Sleeve and side seams, right sides together.

12. Finish the seam allowances as desired and press. Set aside the Bodice.

13. Match the Skirt Front and the Skirt Back at the side seams, right sides together. Pin and sew.

Match Skirt Front and Skirt Back at side seams.

14. Finish the seam allowances as desired. Press.

15. Finish the Skirt Front edges by pressing ¼″ to the wrong side and then another ¼″. Stitch close to the inner folded edge.

Finish Skirt Front edges by pressing to wrong side of fabric ¼″ and then another ¼″.

16. Sew gathering stitches to the top edge of the Skirt, using the method of your choice (see Gathering, page 77).

17. Match the gathered edge of the Skirt to the bottom of the Bodice, right sides together. Pin and sew.

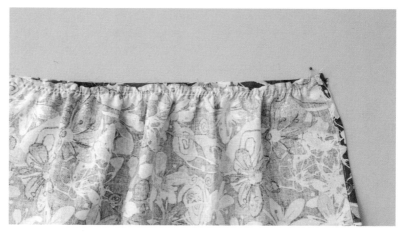

Gather Skirt to Bodice, right sides together.

18. Finish the seam allowances as desired. Press toward the Bodice.

19. Topstitch (page 86) from the right side of the Top/Dress along the Bodice edge, slightly above the Skirt.

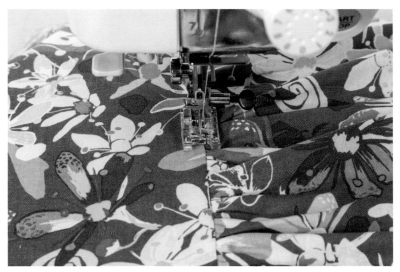

Topstitch above Skirt on Bodice right side.

20. Hem the Sleeves by pressing ¼″ toward the wrong side of the fabric and then another ¼″. Stitch close to the inner folded edge.

21. Hem the Top/Dress by pressing ¼″ toward the wrong side of the fabric and then another ¼″. Stitch close to the inner folded edge.

22. Mark and sew 4 vertical buttonholes ⅝″ from the edge of the left overlap, spacing them evenly and starting and stopping ¼″ from the top edge and Skirt seam.

23. Cut open the buttonholes. Mark the placement of the buttons on the Bodice beneath. Sew the buttons to the Bodice.

24. Hand sew the snap top piece to the inner overlap. Attach the snap bottom piece to the Lining only.

Modern Tunic

This pullover tunic looks great paired with leggings or skinny jeans. Go a little longer for more of a minidress and then add tights and boots. On-seam pockets are a must! (Psst! You can add those pockets to nearly any top/dress or skirt pattern with side seams!)

MATERIALS

- 2½ yards* for Tunic with short sleeves and pockets
- ¼ yard for Yoke lining (can be same as Tunic fabric)
- ⅛ yard ⅛"-wide elastic
- 1 shank button (½")
- Scrap tear-away stabilizer

Yardage will vary based on length chosen.

PREPARING THE PATTERN

1. Trace the appropriate size Bodice Front pattern (pullout page P1) onto pattern paper (see Tracing Patterns, page 86), following the lines for the Tunic Yoke Front. Add ½" to the bottom edge of your pattern for the seam allowance.

2. Trace the Bodice Front below the Tunic Yoke Front line, leaving 15" to the right of the fold line. Add ½" to the top edge for the seam allowance.

3. Extend the new top edge of the Tunic Front 12" to the right.

4. Draw a line perpendicular to the line drawn in Step 3, extending the center front line to the desired length and adding an additional ½" for the hem allowance. Mark this line "Center Front—Cut 1 on fold."

5. Create a new hem by drawing a line at the bottom of the Center Front, extending 3″ past your current side seam.

6. Extend the side seam straight down to the new hem. Measure 2″ to the left and mark.

7. Place a ruler at the top of the side seam, extending down to the mark you just made; draw an angled line. This will be your new side seam.

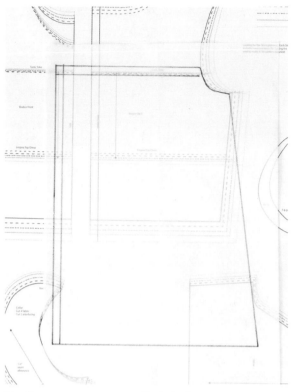

Modify pattern to create new Tunic Back.

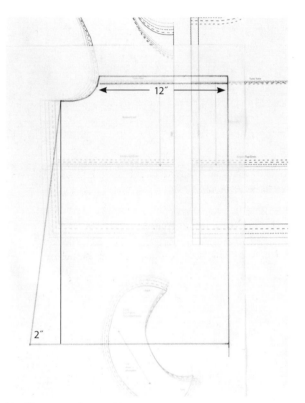

Modify pattern for new Tunic Front.

8. Repeat Steps 1–7 for the Back Bodice piece. Before cutting, match the pattern pieces to make sure that your new side seams and hems align.

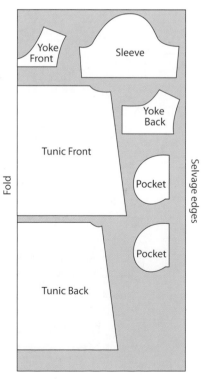

Cutting layout

CUTTING

Yoke

- Cut 1 Yoke Front on fold.
- Cut 2 Yoke Backs.

Sleeves

- Cut 2 Sleeves.

Tunic

- Cut 1 Tunic Front on fold.
- Cut 1 Tunic Back on fold.

Yoke Lining

- Cut 1 Yoke Front on fold.
- Cut 2 Yoke Backs.

Pockets

- Cut 4 Pockets.

CONSTRUCTION

Seam allowances are ½" unless otherwise noted.

1. Match the Yoke Front to the Yoke Backs at the shoulders, right sides together. Pin and sew. Press the seam allowances open.

Match Yoke Front to Yoke Backs at shoulders.

2. Repeat Step 1 with the Yoke lining pieces.

3. Match the Yoke lining to the Yoke exterior at the neckline, right sides together. Pin and sew with ¼" seam allowances. Clip the neckline curves.

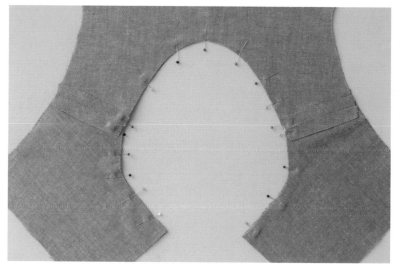

Pin and sew Yoke lining to Yoke exterior at neckline.

4. Press the Lining over the seam allowances and understitch (page 87) the Yoke lining around the neckline.

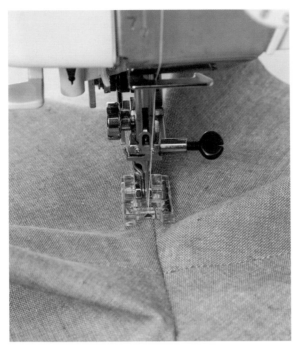

Understitch neckline of Yoke Lining.

5. Cut a 2″ piece of ⅛″ elastic; fold in half to create a loop. Place the elastic loop on the right side (outside) of the left Yoke Back, directly below the neckline seam, matching the raw edges of the elastic loop to the raw edges of the left Yoke Back. Baste the elastic loop in place.

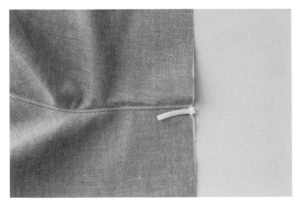

Baste loop of elastic to left Yoke Back.

6. Match the Yoke Back lining to the Yoke Back at the center back raw edges. Pin and sew with ½″ seam allowances.

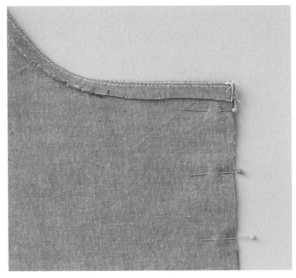

Match Yoke Back lining to Yoke Back.

7. Clip the seam allowances around the neckline (page 76) and at the top of the Bodice Backs.

8. Using a small piece of tear-away stabilizer or tissue paper underneath, match the back edges of the Yoke and baste closed.

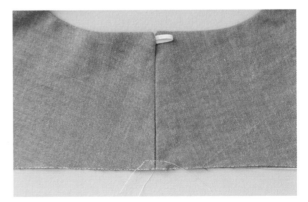

Match back edges of Yoke and baste closed.

9. Baste the Lining and Yoke around the armscye and bottom edges. From this point, you will treat the Yoke as one piece. Set it aside.

10. Finish the raw edges of the Tunic Front and Tunic Back side seams (page 76) and all 4 Pocket pieces.

11. Measure 3″ from the bottom on the side seam of the Tunic Front and mark.

12. Match the bottom edge of 1 Pocket to the mark, aligning the straight edge with the Tunic Front side seams, right sides together. Sew the Pocket to the Tunic Front with a ⅜″ seam allowance.

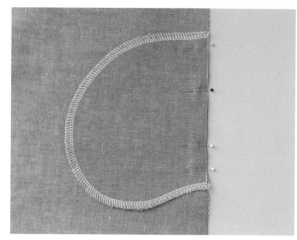

Place Pocket 3″ from bottom of Tunic Front.

13. Press the Pocket over the seam and understitch (page 87) on the Pocket through the seam allowances.

Understitch Pocket.

14. Repeat Steps 11–13 on the opposite side of the Tunic Front with the second Pocket.

15. Follow Steps 11–14 to sew the Pockets to the Tunic Back.

16. Sew gathering stitches (page 77) to the top edge of the Tunic Front ½″ in from each side.

17. Gather the Tunic Front to the front of the Yoke, right sides together. Pin and sew.

Gather Tunic Front to front of Yoke.

18. Press the seam allowances toward the Yoke. From the right side of the Yoke, topstitch (page 86) above the seam, close to the edge.

19. Repeat Steps 17 and 18 with the Tunic Back and the back of the Yoke. Remove the basting stitches and stabilizer.

20. Sew a row of ease stitching (see Ease Stitching, page 76) between the marks on the Sleeve cap.

21. Match the Sleeve and Tunic armscye, right sides together. Pin and sew.

Match Sleeve and Tunic armscye.

22. Finish the seam allowances as desired and press toward the Tunic.

23. Repeat Steps 20–22 with the second Sleeve.

24. With right sides together, match the side seams from the Sleeve to the hem, including the Pockets. Pin and sew, pivoting at the pocket. Press the seam allowances open.

25. Repeat Step 24 with the other side of the Tunic.

26. Hem the bottom edge of the Sleeves by pressing ¼″ to the wrong side of fabric and then another ¼″. Stitch close to the inner folded edge

27. Hem the Tunic by pressing ¼″ to the wrong side of the fabric and then another ½″. Stitch close to the inner folded edge.

28. Sew the button to the back of the yoke, opposite the elastic loop.

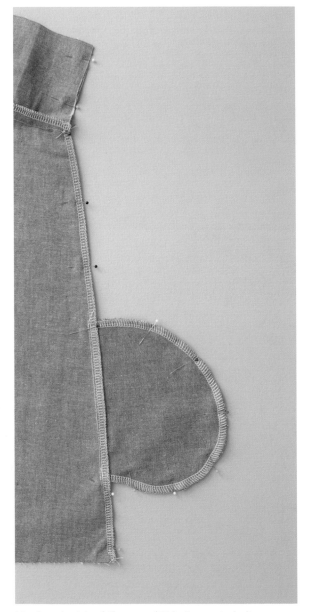

Match underside of Sleeve and Side Seams, including Pockets.

PANTS

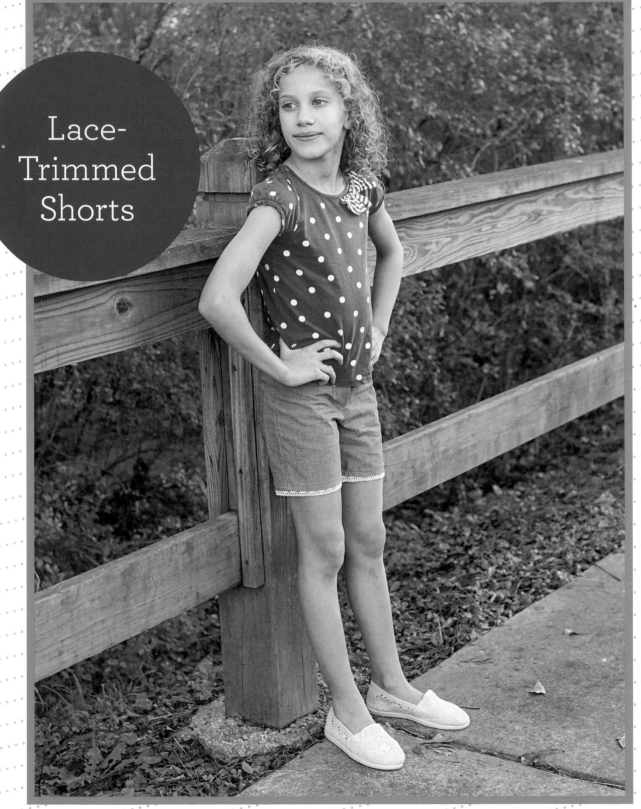

Lace-Trimmed Shorts

Fabric: Chambray by Andover Fabrics

Modern Style for Girls

Living in the steamy South, we're in shorts a big part of the year. The lace adds just enough pizzazz to take these from fun to fabulous. These shorts would also be great made with corduroy without the lace and paired with tights and high-top sneakers for a fall wardrobe staple.

	Size 7	Size 8	Size 9	Size 10	Size 12
Finished inseam length	4½"	5"	5"	5⅛"	5¼"

MATERIALS

- 1 yard for Shorts and Pocket (1¼ yards for size 12)
- ½ yard ¾"-wide buttonhole elastic
- 1¼ yards ½"-wide crocheted lace
- 1 button (¾") for Waistband
- 2 buttons (½") for buttonhole elastic
- 7" zipper

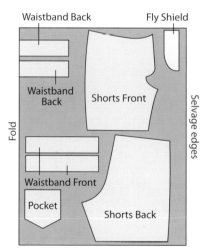

Cutting layout

CUTTING

- Trace the appropriate size of the Front and Back Pants, Pocket, and Fly Shield patterns (pullout page P2) onto pattern paper (see Tracing Patterns, page 86).
- Cut 2 Pants Front, using the Shorts line marked on the pattern.
- Cut 2 Pants Back, using the Shorts line marked on the pattern.
- Cut 2 Pockets.
- Cut 2 Fly Shields.

Cutting continues

All pieces are listed as length × width.

Cut	Size 7	Size 8	Size 9	Size 10	Size 12
Waistband Front (Cut 4: 2 exterior, 2 interior.)	2″ × 9¼″	2″ × 9¾″	2″ × 10″	2″ × 10¼″	2″ × 10¾″
Waistband Back (Cut 2: 1 exterior, 1 interior.)	2″ × 12½″	2″ × 13¼″	2″ × 13½″	2″ × 14″	2″ × 14½″

CONSTRUCTION

Seam allowances are ½″ unless otherwise noted.

1. Finish the raw edges of the Pocket using a serger or zigzag stitch on your sewing machine.

2. Turn and press the top edge of the Pocket ½″ toward the right side of the fabric. Stitch ¼″ from the side edges to secure the hem.

Stitch side edges.

3. Clip the corners of the Pocket and turn right side out. Press.

4. Press the remaining edges of the Pocket ¼″ to the wrong side.

Press edges of Pocket ¼″ to wrong side.

5. Topstitch (page 86) ⅜″ from the top edge of the Pocket.

Topstitch Pocket.

6. Repeat Steps 1–5 with the second Pocket piece.

7. Place the Pocket on the Shorts Back at the line marked on the pattern, with the wrong side of the Pocket against the right side of the Pants. Pin and topstitch the Pocket along the sides and bottom.

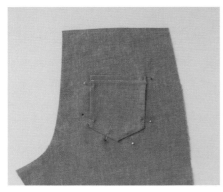

Pin Pocket to Shorts Back.

8. Repeat Step 7 with the second Pocket and Shorts Back.

9. Match a Shorts Front to a Shorts Back along the outer side seam. Pin and sew.

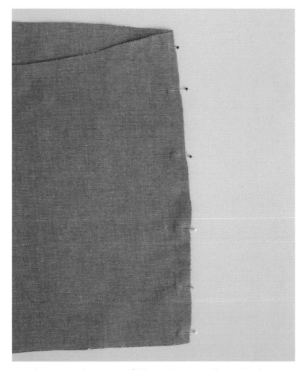

Match outer side seams of Shorts Front to Shorts Back.

10. Finish the seam allowances (see Finishing Seams, page 77) and press.

11. Repeat Steps 9 and 10 with the second Shorts Front and Shorts Back.

12. Match the inseam of the Shorts Front to the Shorts Back. Pin and sew.

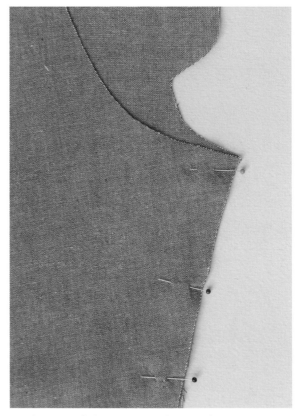

Match inseam of Shorts Front to Shorts Back.

13. Finish the seam allowances as desired and press.

14. Repeat Steps 12 and 13 with the second Shorts Front and Back.

15. Turn a Shorts leg right side out and insert it in the other Shorts leg, right sides together.

16. Match the rise of the Shorts. Pin and sew from the mark below the Fly to the center back Waist.

17. Insert the trouser zipper (page 93).

18. Make and attach the Set-On Waistband (page 89).

19. Mark the buttonhole placement on the Waistband, ½″ in from the side edge of the Waistband and centered vertically.

20. Follow the directions in your sewing machine manual to sew a buttonhole to the Waistband. Use your seam ripper to cut open the buttonhole. Apply a seam sealant such as Fray Check to the buttonhole opening.

21. Mark the placement of the button on the Waistband beneath. Sew a button to the overlapped portion of the Waistband.

22. Fold the hem of one leg of the Shorts ¼″ toward the wrong side of the fabric and press.

23. Match the top edge of the lace to the folded edge of the Shorts, starting at the inseam, and pin. Overlap the lace ¼″. Baste ¼″ from the bottom edge.

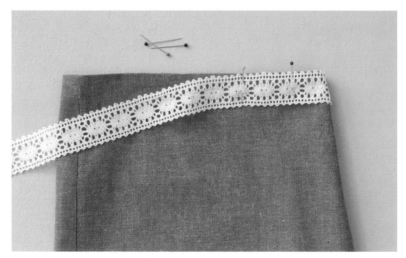

Match and pin lace to hem of Shorts.

24. Fold the bottom edge of the Shorts, including lace, ¼″ toward the wrong side of the fabric. Press. Pin and sew to secure the hem.

25. Repeat Steps 22–24 with the second Shorts leg.

So-Straight Ruffled Pants

I couldn't resist making a more grown-up version of my favorite Ruffled Pants. These have a dainty ruffle as an accent that even my ruffle-averse daughter deemed acceptable. She's also a fan of using a contrasting fabric for the ruffle and pockets.

	Size 7	Size 8	Size 9	Size 10	Size 12
Finished inseam length	23½″	24″	24¾″	25¼″	26½″

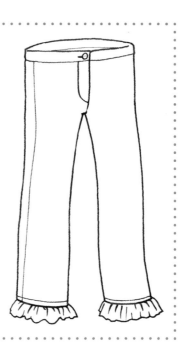

MATERIALS

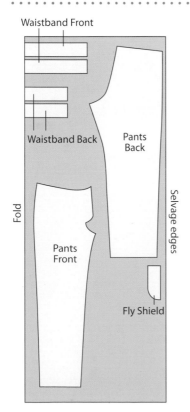

- 2¼ yards for Pants
- ¼ yard for contrasting Ruffle and Pocket (if desired)
- ½ yard ¾″-wide buttonhole elastic
- 1 button (¾″) for Waistband
- 2 buttons (½″) for buttonhole elastic
- 7″ zipper

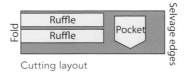

Cutting layout

CUTTING

- Trace the appropriate size of the Front and Back Pants, Pocket, and Fly Shield patterns (pullout page P2) onto pattern paper (see Tracing Patterns, page 86).
- Cut 2 Pants Front.
- Cut 2 Pants Back.
- Cut 2 Pockets.
- Cut 2 Fly Shields.

All pieces are listed as length × width.

Cut	Size 7	Size 8	Size 9	Size 10	Size 12
Ruffle (Cut 2.)	2½″ × 21″	2½″ × 23¾″	2½″ × 24″	2½″ × 25½″	2½″ × 26½″
Waistband Front (Cut 4: 2 exterior, 2 interior.)	2″ × 9¼″	2″ × 9¾″	2″ × 10″	2″ × 10¼″	2″ × 10¾″
Waistband Back (Cut 2: 1 exterior, 1 interior.)	2″ × 12½″	2″ × 13¼″	2″ × 13½″	2″ × 14″	2″ × 14½″

CONSTRUCTION

Seam allowances are ½″ unless otherwise noted.

1. Finish the raw edges of the Pocket, using a serger or zigzag stitch on your sewing machine.

2. Turn the top edge of the Pocket ½″ toward the right side of the fabric. Stitch ¼″ in from the side edges to secure the hem.

Press top edge of Pocket ½″ toward right side of fabric.

3. Clip the corners of the Pocket and turn right side out. Press.

4. Press the remaining edges of the Pocket ¼″ to the wrong side.

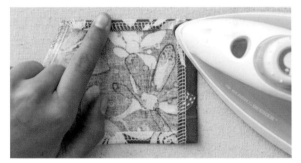

Press edges of Pocket ¼″ to wrong side.

5. Topstitch (page 86) ⅜″ from the top edge of the Pocket.

Topstitch Pocket.

6. Repeat Steps 1–5 with the second Pocket piece.

7. Place the Pocket on the Pants Back at the line marked on the pattern, with the wrong side of the Pocket against the right side of the Pants. Pin and edgestitch the Pocket along the sides and bottom.

Pin Pocket to Pants Back.

8. Repeat Step 7 with the second Pocket and Pants Back.

9. Match a Pants Front to a Pants Back along the outer side seam. Pin and sew.

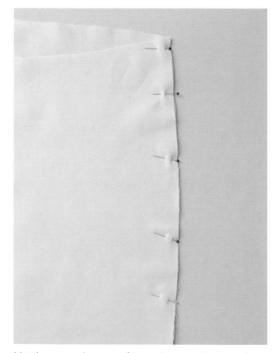

Match outer side seam of Pants Front to Pants Back.

10. Finish the seam allowances as desired (see Finishing Seams, page 77) and press.

11. Repeat Steps 9 and 10 with the second Pants Front and Pants Back.

12. Match the inseam of the Pants Front to the Pants Back. Pin and sew.

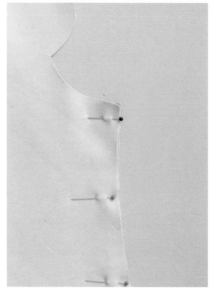

Match inseam of Pants Front to Pants Back.

13. Finish the seam allowance as desired and press.

14. Repeat Steps 12 and 13 with the second Pants Front and Pants Back.

15. Turn a Pants leg right side out and insert it in the other Pants leg, right sides together.

16. Match the rise of the Pants. Pin and sew from the mark below the Fly to the center back Waist.

17. Insert the trouser zipper (page 93).

18. Make and attach the Set-On Waistband (page 89).

19. Mark the buttonhole placement on the Waistband, ½″ from the side edge of the Waistband and centered vertically.

20. Follow the directions in your sewing machine manual to sew a buttonhole to the Waistband. Use your seam ripper to cut open the buttonhole. Apply a seam sealant such as Fray Check to the buttonhole opening.

21. Mark the placement of the button on the Waistband beneath. Sew a button to the over-lapped portion of the Waistband.

22. Match the short edges of the Ruffle. Pin and sew.

Match short edges of Ruffle.

23. Finish the seam allowance and press.

24. Repeat Steps 22 and 23 with the second Ruffle.

25. Hem the Ruffle by pressing the bottom edge ¼″ toward the wrong side and then again ¼″. Topstitch (page 86) close to the inner folded edge.

26. Sew gathering stitches to the top edge of the Ruffle, using the method of your choice (see Gathering, page 77).

27. Place the right side of the Ruffle against the right side of the Pants leg, matching the top edge of the Ruffle to the bottom edge of the Pants. Pin, gather, and sew.

Gather Ruffle to bottom of Pants leg.

28. Finish the seam allowances as desired and press up toward the Pants.

29. Topstitch (page 86) from the right side of the Pants along the bottom edge, slightly above the Ruffle.

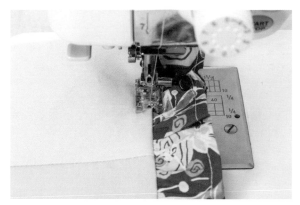

Topstitch Pants leg above Ruffle.

30. Repeat Steps 25–29 with the second Ruffle and Pants leg.

Pedal Pushers

Fabric: Chambray by Andover Fabrics

There's something nostalgic about these cropped pants. I don't know if it's the cool chambray fabric or the vented hems, but I just love them! If you like, you can add pockets to the back or leave them streamlined as shown here.

	Size 7	Size 8	Size 9	Size 10	Size 12
Finished inseam length	15″	15¼″	15¾″	16⅜″	17″

MATERIALS

- 1¾ yards for Pedal Pushers
- ½ yard ¾″-wide buttonhole elastic
- 1 button (¾″) for Waistband
- 2 buttons (½″) for buttonhole elastic
- 7″ zipper

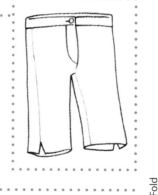

CUTTING

- Trace the appropriate size of the Front and Back Pants and Fly Shield patterns (pullout page P2) onto pattern paper (see Tracing Patterns, page 86).
- Cut 2 Pants Front, using the Pedal Pushers line marked on the pattern.
- Cut 2 Pants Back, using the Pedal Pushers line marked on the pattern.
- Cut 2 Fly Shields.

....

Cutting continues

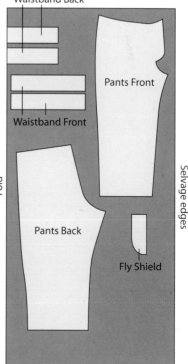

Waistband Back

Pants Front

Waistband Front

Fold

Pants Back

Fly Shield

Selvage edges

Cutting layout

All pieces are listed as length × width.

Cut	Size 7	Size 8	Size 9	Size 10	Size 12
Waistband Front (Cut 4: 2 exterior, 2 interior.)	2″ × 9¼″	2″ × 9¾″	2″ × 10″	2″ × 10¼″	2″ × 10¾″
Waistband Back (Cut 2: 1 exterior, 1 interior.)	2″ × 12½″	2″ × 13¼″	2″ × 13½″	2″ × 14″	2″ × 14½″

CONSTRUCTION

Seam allowances are ½″ unless otherwise noted.

1. Finish the outer side seam allowance edges, if desired.

2. Match a Pants Front to a Pants Back along the outer side seam, stopping 2″ above the hem. Pin and sew.

3. Press the seam allowances open, continuing down to the hem, so that the unsewn portion of the Pants leg is pressed ½″ to the wrong side of the fabric.

4. From the right side of the Pants leg, top-stitch (page 86) ⅜″ away from the vent. Pivot and stitch perpendicular to the vent. Pivot and continue sewing along the other side of the vent to the hem.

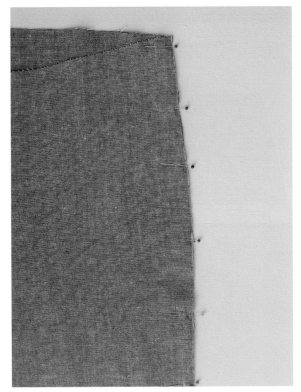

Match outer side seam of Pants Front to Pants Back.

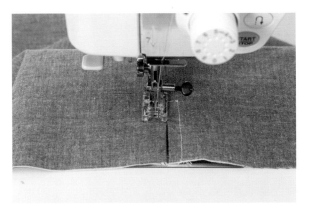

Topstitch hem vent on outside of each Pants leg.

5. Repeat Steps 2–4 with the second Pants Front and Pants Back.

6. Match the inseam of the Pants Front to the Pants Back. Pin and sew.

7. Finish the seam allowances as desired (see Finishing Seams, page 77) and press.

8. Repeat Steps 6 and 7 with the second Pants Front and Back.

9. Turn a Pants leg right side out and insert it in the other Pants leg, right sides together.

10. Match the rise of the Pants. Pin and sew from the mark below the Fly to the center back Waist.

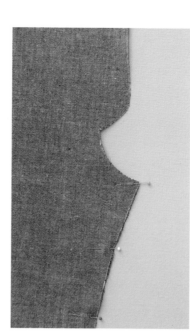

Match inseam of Pants Front to Pants Back.

11. Insert the trouser zipper (page 93).

12. Make and attach the Set-On Waistband (page 89).

13. Mark the buttonhole placement on the Waistband, ½″ in from the side edge of the Waistband and centered vertically.

14. Follow the directions in your sewing machine manual to sew a buttonhole to the Waistband. Use your seam ripper to cut open the buttonhole. Apply a seam sealant such as Fray Check to the buttonhole opening.

15. Mark the placement of the button on the Waistband beneath. Sew a button to the overlapped portion of the Waistband.

16. Hem the Pants by pressing the bottom edge ¼″ toward the wrong side and then again ¼″. Topstitch (page 86) close to the inner folded edge.

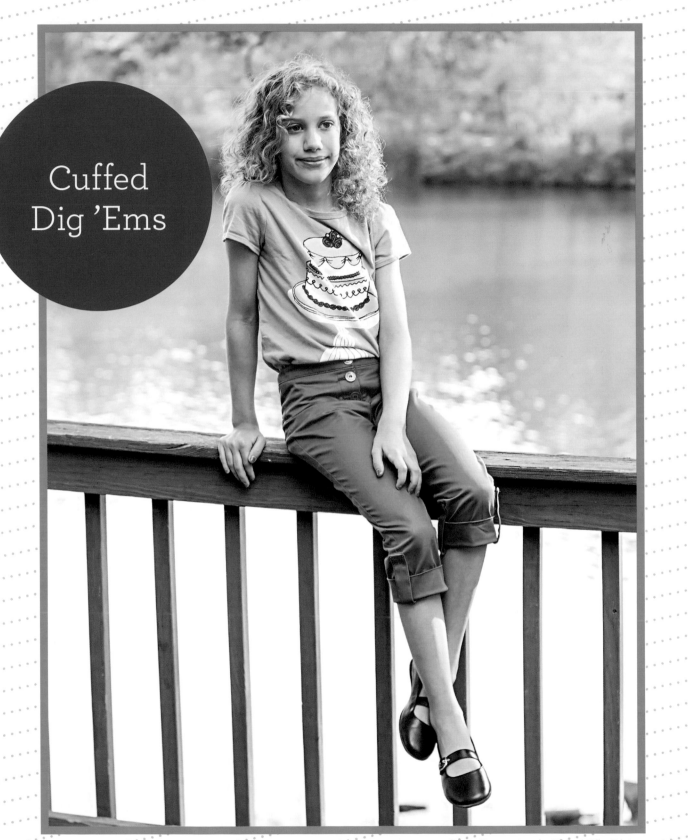

Cuffed
Dig 'Ems

Fabric: Cotton sateen by Michael Miller Fabrics.

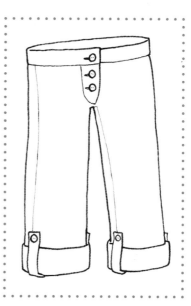

I wanted to change things up a bit. These stylish Cuffed Dig 'Ems feature a button fly and give you the opportunity to add contrasting topstitching and other fun details to truly reflect your tween.

	Size 7	Size 8	Size 9	Size 10	Size 12
Finished inseam length	16″	16½″	16¾″	17½″	18¼″

MATERIALS

- 2¼ yards for Cuffed Dig 'Ems, Straps, Cuffs, and Pockets
- ½ yard ¾″-wide buttonhole elastic
- 7 buttons (¾″) for Waistband, Fly, and Straps
- 2 buttons (½″), for buttonhole elastic

CUTTING

- Trace the appropriate size of the Front and Back Pants, Pocket, and Fly Shield patterns (pullout page P2) onto pattern paper (see Tracing Patterns, page 86).
- Cut 2 Pants Front, using the Cuffed Dig 'Ems line marked on the pattern.
- Cut 2 Pants Back, using the Cuffed Dig 'Ems line marked on the pattern.
- Cut 2 Pockets.
- Cut 2 Fly Shields.
- Cut 4 Straps 4″ × 8″.

Cutting continues

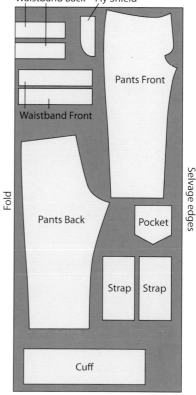

Cutting layout

All pieces are listed as length × width.

Cut	Size 7	Size 8	Size 9	Size 10	Size 12
Cuffs (Cut 2.)	4″ × 12⅞″	4″ × 13¼″	4″ × 13¾″	4″ × 14½″	4″ × 15″
Waistband Front (Cut 4: 2 exterior, 2 interior.)	2″ × 9¼″	2″ × 9¾″	2″ × 10″	2″ × 10¼″	2″ × 10¾″
Waistband Back (Cut 2: 1 exterior, 1 interior.)	2″ × 12½″	2″ × 13¼″	2″ × 13½″	2″ × 14″	2″ × 14½″

CONSTRUCTION

Seam allowances are ½″ unless otherwise noted.

1. Finish the raw edges of the Pocket, using a serger or zigzag stitch on your sewing machine.

2. Turn the top edge of the Pocket ½″ toward the right side of the fabric. Stitch ¼″ from the side edges to secure the hem.

3. Clip the corners of the Pocket and turn right side out. Press.

4. Press the remaining edges of the Pocket ¼″ to the wrong side.

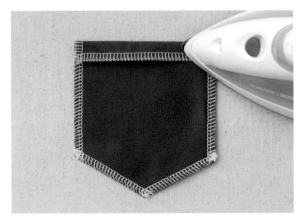

Press top edge of Pocket ½″ toward right side of fabric.

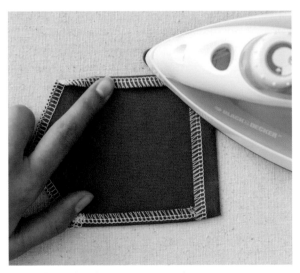

Press edges of Pocket ¼″ to wrong side.

5. Topstitch (page 86) ⅜″ from the top edge of the Pocket.

Topstitch Pocket.

6. Repeat Steps 1–5 with the second Pocket piece.

7. Place the Pocket on the Pants Back at the line marked on the pattern, with the wrong side of the Pocket to the right side of the Pants. Pin and topstitch (page 86) the Pocket along the sides and bottom.

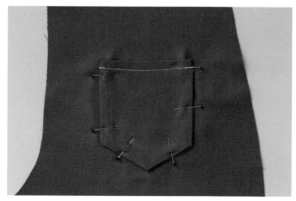

Pin Pocket to Pants Back.

8. Repeat Step 7 with the second Pocket and Pants Back.

9. Press the Strap in half, wrong sides together, matching the long edges.

10. Open the Strap and press the raw edges to the wrong side, matching the long edges to the crease pressed in Step 9.

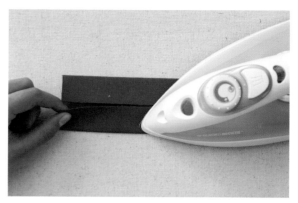

Press raw edges of Strap to wrong side.

11. Fold the Strap in half, right sides together, so the raw long edges are visible. Pin and sew across the short edges with a ¼″ seam allowance.

Fold Strap in half, right sides together.

12. Trim the corners and turn the Strap right side out. Press and topstitch along both long edges.

13. Repeat Steps 9–12 with the 3 remaining Straps.

14. Match a Pants Front to a Pants Back along the outer side seam. Pin and sew.

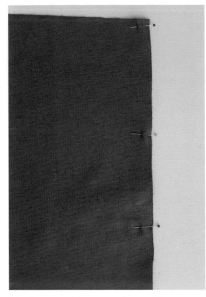

Match outer side seam of Pants Front to Pants Back.

15. Finish the seam allowances (see Finishing Seams, page 77) and press.

16. Make a mark 4″ from the hem along the outer side seam on the wrong side of the Pants Leg.

17. Center a Strap over the seam, with the top edge even with the mark from Step 16. Sew a 1″ square to secure the Strap to the Pants (box seam).

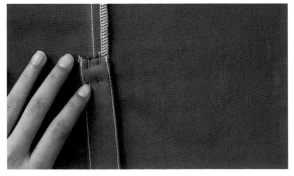

Center Strap over seam, with top edge even with mark.

18. Repeat Steps 16 and 17 with the second Pants Front, Pants Back, and Strap.

19. Match the inseam of the Pants Front to the Pants Back. Pin and sew.

Match inseam of Pants Front to Pants Back.

20. Finish the seam allowance as desired and press.

21. Repeat Steps 16 and 17 to add Straps to the inseam of the Pants.

22. Match the short edges of the Cuff. Pin and sew.

Match short edges of Cuff.

23. Press the seam allowances open.

24. Press the Cuff, wrong sides together, matching the raw edges.

25. Pin the raw edge of the Cuff to the bottom edge of the Pants, matching the Cuff seam to the inner Pants Leg seam. Make sure the Straps are tucked out of the way (so you don't accidently get them caught in your stitching).

Pin Cuff to bottom of Pants Leg.

26. Sew the Cuff. Finish the seam allowances as desired and press toward the Pants.

27. Topstitch from the right side of the Pants along the bottom edge, slightly above the Cuff.

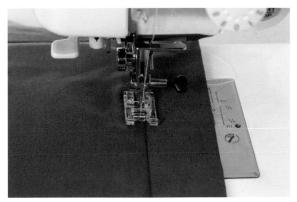

Topstitch Pants Leg above Cuff.

28. Roll up the Cuff, over the Pants.

29. Repeat Steps 22–28 with the second Cuff and Pants Leg.

30. Pull the Strap over the Cuff and match with the box seam used in Step 17 to attach the Strap to the inside of the Pants Leg. Pin and sew.

Match Strap to box seam on right side of Pants Leg.

31. Repeat Step 30 with the remaining 3 straps.

32. Turn a Pants Leg wrong side out and insert the other Pants Leg into it, right sides together.

33. Match the rise of the Pants. Pin and sew from the mark below the Fly to the center back Waist.

34. Follow the instructions for the Trouser Zipper (page 93) to attach the Fly Shield and finish the Fly Facing, but omit the zipper.

35. Make and attach the Set-On Waistband (page 89).

36. Mark the buttonhole placement on the Waistband, ½″ in from the side edge of the Waistband and centered vertically. Mark 2 additional buttonholes on the Fly Facing, ½″ in from the side edge and spaced evenly.

Mark buttonholes on Waistband and Fly Facing.

37. Follow the directions in your sewing machine manual to sew buttonholes to the Waistband and Fly Facing. Use your seam ripper to cut open the buttonholes. Apply a seam sealant such as Fray Check to the buttonhole opening.

38. Mark the placement of the buttons on the Waistband and Fly Shield beneath. Sew the buttons to the overlapped portion of the Waistband and Fly Shield, as well as the tops of each Strap.

SKIRTS

Beyond Borders Skirt

Fabrics: Kawaii Asian Collection by Robert Kaufman Fabrics

This has been one of my daughter's favorite skirts to wear. She loves it with T-shirts and sandals in warmer months and leggings or tights and boots during cooler weather. Mix it up by adding a touch of lace to the hem or eliminating the ruffle altogether.

	Size 7/8	Size 9/10	Size 12
Finished length	17″	20¾″	23¾″

MATERIALS

- ¾ yard for Yoke
- 1⅝ yards for Lower Skirt
- ⅜ yard for Ruffle
- 1 yard ¾″-wide nonroll elastic

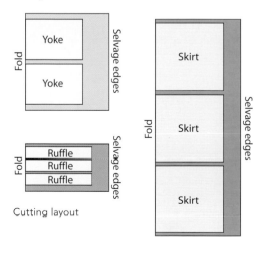

Cutting layout

CUTTING

All pieces are listed as length × width.

Cut	Size 7/8	Size 9/10	Size 12
Yoke (Cut 2.)	7½″ × 25½″	8¾″ × 27″	10″ × 28¾″
Lower Skirt (Cut 3.)	12½″ × 29½″	15″ × 31½″	16¾″ × 33½″
Ruffle (Cut 3.)	3″ × 29½″	3″ × 31½″	3″ × 33½″

CONSTRUCTION

Seam allowances are ½" unless otherwise noted.

1. Place the 2 rectangles for the Yoke right sides together. Pin and sew along the short sides.

2. Place 2 Lower Skirt rectangles right sides together. Pin and sew together along a short side. Add the third Lower Skirt rectangle to create a continuous circle. Set aside.

3. Place 2 Ruffle strips right sides together. Pin and sew together along a short side. Add the third Ruffle strip to create a continuous circle.

Create Ruffle by sewing 3 rectangles together at short edges.

4. Finish the seam allowances as desired (see Finishing Seams, page 77). Press all 3 pieces.

5. Hem the Ruffle by pressing the bottom edge ¼" toward the wrong side and then again ¼". Topstitch (page 86) close to the inner folded edge.

6. Hem the Lower Skirt by pressing the bottom edge ¼" toward the wrong side and then again ½". Topstitch close to the inner folded edge.

7. Sew gathering stitches to the top edge of the Ruffle and Lower Skirt, using the method of your choice (see Gathering, page 77).

8. Place the right side of the Ruffle against the right side of the Yoke, matching the top edge of the Ruffle to the bottom edge of the Yoke. Pin, gather, and baste with a ⅜" seam allowance.

Baste Ruffle to bottom edge of Yoke.

9. Match the gathered edge of the Lower Skirt to the Ruffle/Yoke piece from Step 8. Pin and sew.

10. Finish the seam allowances (Yoke, Ruffle, and Lower Skirt) as desired. Press toward the Yoke.

11. Topstitch from the right side of the skirt along the Yoke edge, slightly above the Ruffle and Lower Skirt.

12. Create a Waistband casing and insert the elastic (see Waistbands, page 87).

Paneled No-Hem Skirt

Fabrics: Hedgehog Meadow and Emmeline by Michael Miller Fabrics; Gypsy Bandana by Pillow & Maxfield for Michael Miller Fabrics

*M*ake this skirt super scrappy by using as many fabrics as there are pieces, or go for a more subdued look by limiting your fabric selection.

	Size 7/8	Size 9/10	Size 12
Finished length	17″	21″	25″

MATERIALS

- ¾ yard for Yoke
- 6 fat quarters for Panels
- ¾ yard for Hem Band
- 1 yard ¾″-wide nonroll elastic

CUTTING

All pieces are listed as length × width.

Cut	Size 7/8	Size 9/10	Size 12
Yoke (Cut 2.)	6½″ × 25½″	7¾″ × 27″	9″ × 28¾″
Panels (Cut 6.)	10¾″ × 15¼″	13½″ × 16¼″	16¼″ × 17¼″
Hem Band (Cut 3.)	6″ × 29½″	6″ × 31½″	6″ × 33½″

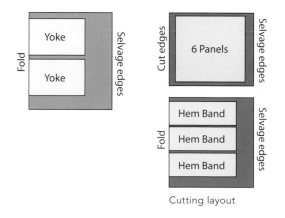

Cutting layout

CONSTRUCTION

Seam allowances are ½" unless otherwise noted.

1. Place the 2 rectangles for the Yoke right sides together. Pin and sew along the short sides.

2. Place 2 Panels right sides together. Pin and sew along a short edge. Repeat this step until all 6 Panels are sewn together in a continuous circle.

Sew Panels together to create lower portion of skirt.

3. Finish the seam allowances as desired (see Finishing Seams, page 77). Press the Yoke and Panels.

4. Place 2 Hem Band pieces right sides together. Pin and sew together along a short side. Add the third Hem Band piece to create a continuous circle.

5. Press the seam allowances open on the Hem Band. Match the long edge of the Hem Band and press, wrong sides together, to create a piece 3″ × the width of the bottom edge of the Panels.

Press Hem Band in half, wrong sides together, to prepare it for attaching to bottom edge of Panels.

6. Match the raw edges of the Hem Band to the lower edge of the Panels, right sides together. Pin and sew, finishing the seam allowances as desired. Press toward the Panels.

7. Topstitch (page 86) on the right side of the Panels above the hem band seam.

8. Sew gathering stitches to the top edge of the Panels, using the method of your choice (see Gathering, page 77).

9. Place the right side of the Panels against the right side of the Yoke, matching the raw edges of the Panels to the bottom edge of the Yoke. Pin, gather, and sew.

Match gathered Panels to bottom edge of Yoke.

10. Finish the seam allowances (Yoke and Panels) as desired. Press toward the Yoke.

11. Topstitch from the right side of the skirt along the Yoke edge, slightly above the Panels.

12. Create a Waistband casing in the Yoke and insert the elastic (see Waistbands, page 87).

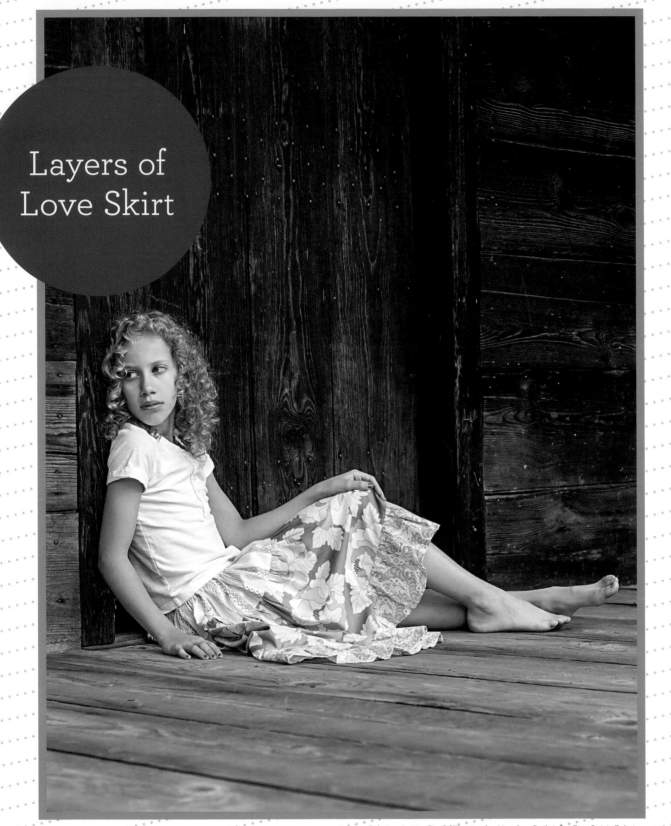

Layers of
Love Skirt

Fabrics: Lottie Da Collection by Heather Bailey for FreeSpirit Fabrics

My daughter still loves "twirly" skirts, and this one remains a wardrobe staple for her. It's a bit longer than the other skirts, which makes it a little more immune to those unexpected growth spurts.

	Size 7/8	Size 9/10	Size 12
Finished length	21″	24″	29″

MATERIALS

- ⅝ yard for Tier 1
- 1½ yards for Tier 2
- 1¼ yards for Tier 3
- 1 yard ¾″-wide nonroll elastic

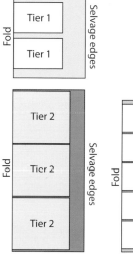

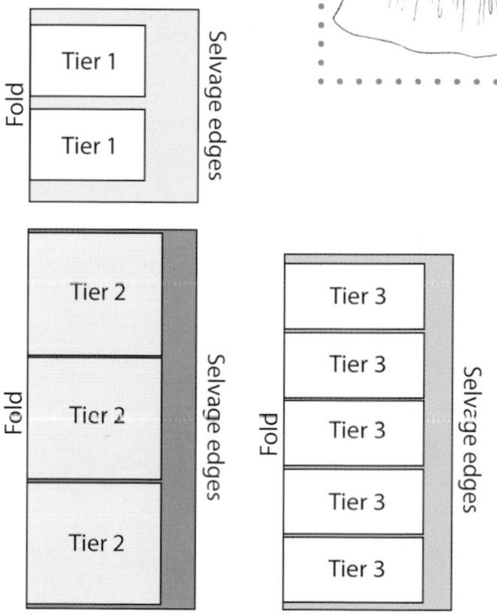

Cutting layout

CUTTING

All pieces are listed as length × width.

Cut	Size 7/8	Size 9/10	Size 12
Tier 1 (Cut 2.)	7″ × 25½″	7¾″ × 27″	9″ × 28¾″
Tier 2 (Cut 3.)	11½″ × 29½″	13″ × 31½″	15½″ × 33½″
Tier 3 (Cut 4 for sizes 7/8 and 9/10; cut 5 for size 11/12.)	6¼″ × 38½″	7″ × 41″	8¼″ × 35″

CONSTRUCTION

Seam allowances are ½" unless otherwise noted.

1. Place the 2 rectangles for Tier 1 right sides together. Pin and sew along the short sides.

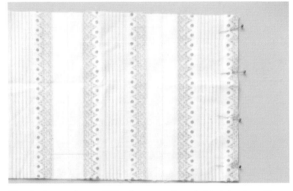

Match short edges of Tier 1 rectangles, right sides together.

2. Place 2 rectangles for Tier 2 right sides together. Pin and sew together along a short side. Add the third Tier 2 rectangle to create a continuous circle. Set aside.

Match short edges of Tier 2 rectangles, right sides together.

3. Place 2 rectangles for Tier 3 right sides together. Pin and sew together along a short side. Add the remaining Tier 3 rectangles to create a continuous circle. Set aside.

Match short edges of Tier 3 rectangles, right sides together.

4. Finish the seam allowances (see Finishing Seams, page 77). Press all 3 tiers.

5. Hem Tier 3 by pressing the bottom edge ¼" toward the wrong side and then again ½". Topstitch (page 86) close to the inner folded edge.

6. Sew gathering stitches to the top edges of Tier 2 and Tier 3, using the method of your choice (see Gathering, page 77).

7. Match the top edge of Tier 3 to the bottom edge of Tier 2, right sides together. Pin, gather, and sew.

Gather and sew Tier 3 to bottom of Tier 2.

8. Finish the seam allowances as desired. Press toward Tier 2.

9. Topstitch from the right side of the skirt along the Tier 2 edge, slightly above Tier 3.

Topstitch above Tier 3.

10. Match the top edge of Tier 2 to the bottom edge of Tier 1, right sides together. Pin, gather, and sew.

Gather and sew Tier 2 to Tier 1.

11. Finish the seam allowances as desired and press toward Tier 1.

12. Topstitch on the right side of the skirt along the Tier 1 edge, slightly above Tier 2.

Topstitch above Tier 2.

13. Create a Waistband casing and insert the elastic (see Waistbands, page 87).

Kicky Pleated Skirt

Aflat-front waistband and box pleats make for a slightly more mature look that's still age appropriate for a young lady. It's also super fast to sew!

	Size 7/8	Size 9/10	Size 12
Finished length	16″	20″	24″

MATERIALS

- 1⅝ yards of fabric
- ⅛ yard midweight fusible interfacing
- ½ yard ¾″-wide nonroll elastic
- 4 buttons (¾″)

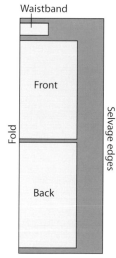

Waistband

Fold

Front

Back

Selvage edges

Cutting layout

CUTTING

All pieces are listed as length × width.

Cut	Size 7/8	Size 9/10	Size 12
Front (Cut 1.)	16½″ × 25½″	20½″ × 27″	24½″ × 28¾″
Back (Cut 1.)	18¼″ × 25½″	22¼″ × 27″	26¼″ × 28¾″
Waistband (Cut 1.)	3½″ × 13″	3½″ × 13½″	3½″ × 14″

CONSTRUCTION

Seam allowances are ½″ unless otherwise noted.

1. Mark pleats on the Skirt Front by measuring from each side, using the following measurements:

Mark	Size 7/8	Size 9/10	Size 12
Mark 1	3¾″	3¼″	3½″
Mark 2	6⅞″	6¾″	7¼″
Mark 3	10″	10¼″	10⅞″

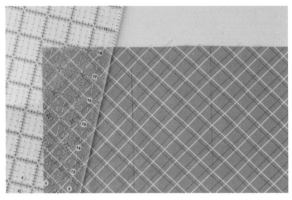

Mark pleats on Skirt Front.

2. Press on Mark 1 and Mark 3 to create the pleat lines, wrong sides together.

3. Match the pleats to Mark 2, forming a box pleat. Press well.

Match pleats to Mark 2.

4. Stitch close to the inside edge of the box pleat, stopping ¾″ from the bottom. Repeat this step with the 3 remaining box pleat inside edges.

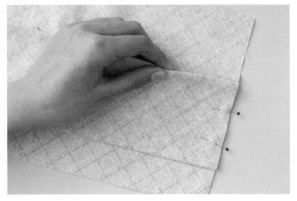

Edgestitch inner edge of box pleat.

5. Measure and mark 4″ from the top edge of the Skirt Front. Repeat this step with the second pleat.

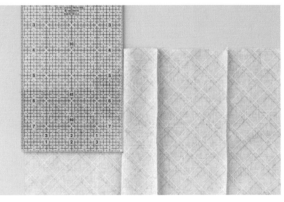

Measure 4″ along edge of pleat.

6. Match the outer pleats, right sides together. Pin and sew from the top edge to the mark. Repeat this step with the second pleat.

7. Press the pleats flat. Baste the top edge of the Skirt Front.

8. Finish the side edges as desired (see Finishing Edges, page 76). Set aside.

9. Press the top edge of the Skirt Back ¼″ to the wrong side of the fabric and then another 1″.

10. Stitch close to the inner folded edge to create a Waistband casing (see Waistbands, page 87).

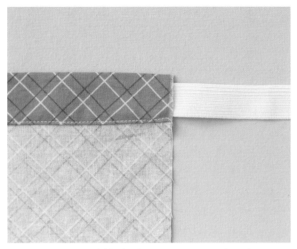

Sew close to inner folded edge to create Waistband casing.

11. Cut a piece of ¾″ elastic equal to half of your child's waist measurement. Use a bodkin or safety pin to feed the elastic through the casing.

12. When the free end of the elastic is even with the opening of the casing, pin it in place. Baste across the elastic to secure.

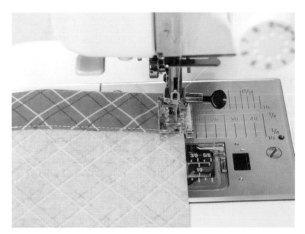

Baste across ends of elastic to secure.

13. Continue pulling the elastic through the casing. Make sure your elastic lays flat within the Waistband casing. Remove the bodkin or safety pin and pin the elastic edges in place. Baste across the edges to secure the elastic.

14. Finish the side seams of the Skirt Back as desired. Set aside.

15. Follow the manufacturer's directions to fuse interfacing to the wrong side of the Waistband.

16. Press the Waistband in half, wrong sides together, matching the long edges.

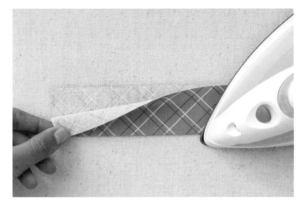

Press Waistband in half, wrong sides together.

17. Press a raw edge of the Waistband ½″ toward the wrong side.

Press 1 raw edge of Waistband ½″ toward wrong side.

18. Match the unpressed raw edges of the Waistband to the Skirt Front, right sides together. Pin and sew. Press the seam allowances toward the Waistband.

Match raw edge of Waistband to Skirt Front, right sides together.

19. Match the side of the Skirt Back to the Skirt Front, right sides together.

20. Fold the Waistband in half, right sides together, matching the folded edge of the Waistband to the seam above the Skirt Front. The elastic casing should be in the middle of the Waistband. Pin and sew. Clip the top corner of the side seam to reduce the bulk.

Fold Waistband over elastic casing, right sides together.

21. Repeat Steps 19 and 20 with the other side seam of the Skirt.

22. Turn the Waistband right side out. Press.

23. Pin the inner edge of the Waistband. Topstitch (page 86) from the front of the Skirt along the bottom edge of the Waistband.

Pin Waistband.

24. Hem the Skirt by pressing the bottom edge ¼″ toward the wrong side and then again ¼″. Topstitch close to the inner folded edge.

25. Position the buttons on the center front of the Skirt, ¼″ from the pleat seams. Sew the buttons to the Skirt Front by hand.

Place buttons on center front of Skirt.

Techniques A–Z

Here's a basic dictionary of terms and techniques commonly used in sewing clothing. With each technique, a brief "tutorial" provides how-to specifics. Many of the projects refer to techniques in this section; you may find it helpful to bookmark ones that are unfamiliar, so you can locate them easily while sewing.

BACKSTITCH

This machine stitch locks in the starting and ending stitches of a seam. At the beginning and end of each seam, sew forward three or four stitches. Use the reverse button or lever on your sewing machine to sew back along that line for three or four stitches. Release the button and continue sewing. End each seam by back-stitching three or four stitches.

BASTING

Basting stitches are used to hold two or more pieces of fabric in place before you sew a seam. Basting allows you to test fit and placement before you do the final stitching. Set your sewing machine to the longest stitch length and move your needle position so you are sewing as close to the edge as possible. In this book, you'll encounter basting when making the Wrap Top/Dress and when assembling tiered skirts.

BUTTONHOLE

A buttonhole consists of two parallel lines of tight zigzag stitches with end pieces (bar tacks) of wider zigzag stitching. Check your sewing machine manual for the available buttonhole stitches and the steps needed for your specific machine.

Note: *To stabilize the fabric where the buttonhole will go, it's essential that you press fusible interfacing onto the fabric's wrong side.*

Basting stitches

Sew basting stitches inside seam allowances.

Your sewing machine manual includes instructions for sewing buttonholes.

CURVES

When you sew a curved seam such as an armhole, get in the habit of keeping your eye on the presser foot and *not* on the sewing needle. Just take it slow and steady, guiding the fabric from in front of the presser foot without pushing it forward. It's okay to raise the presser foot and adjust the fabric on tight curves, but make sure that when you do, the needle is in the down position, through the fabric, so it doesn't shift.

After stitching, curves are typically notched or clipped so the seam will lie properly after turning a garment right side out. This technique will be used on the garments sewn in the Basic Bodice chapter.

When you clip concave curves such as armholes, carefully use the tip of your scissors to snip the fabric of the seam allowance perpendicular to your stitches. Take care not to snip through the stitches. Space your cuts about ⅓″ apart through the curve.

On convex curves, cut triangular notches out of the seam allowance.

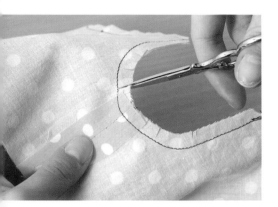

Clip through seam allowance just to stitches on concave curves.

EASE STITCHING

Ease stitching is one row of long straight stitches within the seam allowance. Ease stitching the caps of the sleeves will help them fit into the armscyes.

FINISHING EDGES

Use a serger or tight zigzag stitch close to the edges to keep them from fraying.

FINISHING SEAMS

With all the work you put into making a garment, you want it to hold up through wearing, washing, and drying. One of the best ways to do that is by finishing your seams. The fastest way, in my opinion, is with a serger, but it's far from the only or cheapest way. You can use pinking shears to cut along the raw edges of the seam allowance, then press seams open. Or you can sew a line of wide zigzag stitches along the edge of each piece of fabric before sewing the pieces together. After sewing the seams, press them open.

Serged seam

Pinked seam

Zigzag-stitched seam

GATHERING

This remains one of my most-used sewing skills when making garments. I'll sometimes cheat and set up my serger to gather (consult your serger's manual for instructions on how to gather ruffles using a serger), but it's never as precise as the methods described here.

The steps that follow describe making gathered tiers from rectangles of fabric and sewing them around the bottom of a skirt or dress or pants legs. Before gathering, the short ends of the ruffle pieces are sewn together to make a continuous circle.

TIP

My friend, Angela Shimada, taught me to sew the front and back gathering stitches separately, with the four rows meeting at the side seams. It's so much easier to do it this way than to have two long rows that go all the way around a ruffle (especially when it's the bottom tier of a ruffled skirt).

Traditional Method

1. Set your sewing machine stitch length to the longest stitch and move the needle position all the way to the right. (If you have an older sewing machine, move the fabric to sew within the ½″ seam allowance.) Along the edge of the ruffle strip between 2 seams, sew 2 parallel rows of stitches—inside the seam allowance, about ¼″ apart—from one side seam to the other. Do not backstitch at the beginning and end of each row, and be careful that your rows of stitches do not cross each other. You also should leave about 4″ to 6″ of thread tail, which you'll pull to gather the fabric.

Sew 2 parallel lines of stitches within seam allowance.

2. On the bottom edge of the piece to which you are attaching the ruffle, mark the center point between the seams on each side. Do the same on the piece you are gathering. Match these 4 points and pin them together, lining up the raw edges, with the fabric right sides together.

3. Pull the tail ends of thread at a side seam to begin gathering the fabric. Use your fingers to slide the gathers toward the middle point of your ruffle; check frequently to see if the gathered section fits the flat section below it. Distribute the gathers evenly along the area and pin to hold them in place. Continue with the other 3 quadrants until the entire piece is gathered and pinned.

4. Use a regular stitch length and seam allowance to sew the pieces together. I sew a little slowly and remove the pins before they slide under the presser foot. It helps to position the fabric gathers before they go under the foot, so the gathering is stitched neatly into the seam. Otherwise, you can end up with wonky-looking gathers.

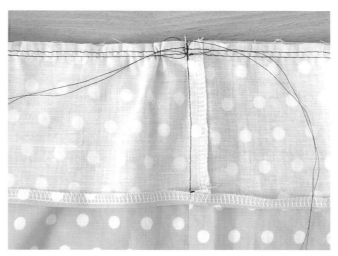
Match seams and center points on each side of ruffle.

Pull threads and distribute gathers evenly.

Pin and then sew the ruffle.

Zigzag Method

1. Set your sewing machine to its widest zigzag stitch. Cut a piece of narrow ribbon, yarn, or embroidery floss slightly longer than the ruffle. Place the ribbon within the seam allowance of the ruffle. Center the presser foot over the ribbon; check the width of the zigzag to make sure it won't catch the ribbon. Zigzag over the ribbon from one side seam to the other, being careful not to catch the ribbon in the stitches. Repeat on the other side of your piece.

Sew wide zigzag stitch over ribbon, yarn, or embroidery floss.

2. Repeat the Traditional Method, Steps 2–4 (page 78), to mark, pin, gather, and stitch the ruffle to the garment piece. After sewing, remove the ribbon or yarn.

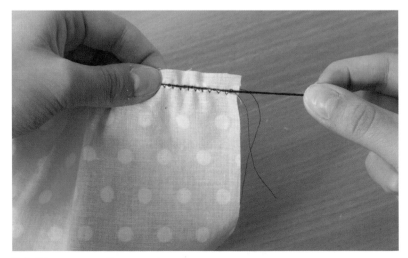

Pull ribbon, yarn, or floss to make gathers.

HEMS

Most of the projects in this book call for a machine-stitched hem. I use a serger to finish the edges of my garments, but a turned hem looks even better, in my opinion. With the garment wrong side out, simply fold the hem ¼″ toward the wrong side and press. Turn another ¼″ or ½″ and press. Stitch close to the inside hem edge. I line up the bottom edge with the right side of my presser foot and move the needle all the way over to the right. If you are not able to move the needle on your sewing machine, adjust your fabric so you can sew more closely to the inner folded edge. Use a medium stitch length (3 on my machine) to stitch.

TIP

I'm always looking for easier ways to do things, so my cheater way of turning a hem is to run a line of basting stitches ¼″ from the bottom edge, all the way around the hem. I then use that row of stitches as my guide for turning and pressing the hem. Because the stitching will be on the inside of the garment, it's not necessary to remove it.

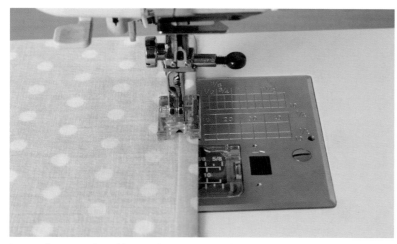

Line up bottom edge of hem with your presser foot to help keep your stitches even.

MATCHING SEAMS

When sewing together pieces across seams, match the seams first and pin in place; then insert pins in between the seams. You'll want to do this on nearly all of the Basic Bodice patterns, as well as some of the Skirt patterns.

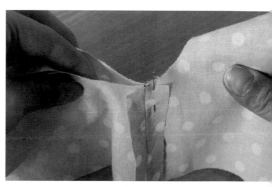

Start pinning pieces together by matching seams first.

PATTERN AND FABRIC LAYOUT

Before laying out your pattern, match the selvage edges of your fabric and make sure there are no creases or wrinkles. Lay it on a flat surface in preparation for cutting. (Refer to Tracing Patterns, page 86, for information on preparing the patterns in this book.) Check the pattern pieces for a long arrow to indicate the direction of the grain. The arrow should run parallel to the selvage of the fabric. If the piece is to be placed on a fold, the fold should be parallel to the selvage unless otherwise indicated.

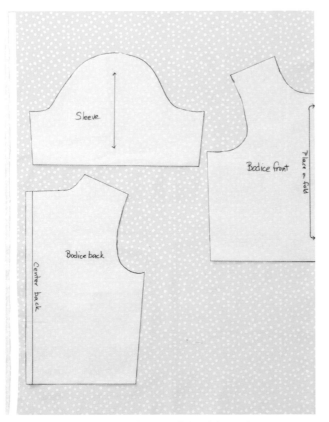

Lay pattern pieces with grainline parallel to fabric selvage.

Use pattern weights or a few pins to hold the pattern to the fabric while you cut it with scissors or a rotary cutter. The fabric and pattern should stay as flat as possible while you cut. Don't lift up the fabric to cut around it. I try to cut near the corner of a table so I can move around the fabric and have access to nearly all sides.

Note: *Sometimes the pattern pieces will be turned face down to match the cutting layouts and make better use of the fabrics.*

PRESSER FEET

For sewing garments, I prefer to use a clear appliqué foot. It allows me to really see what I'm sewing, since the traditional straight-stitch foot is all metal. The clear foot is great for topstitching. I can line up the seam that I will be sewing above so it's right along the inside edge of the foot, tap my needle position over to the right, and stitch as close as I want with nothing obstructing my view.

PINNING

Insert pins perpendicular to the edge of the seam so that, as you stitch, you can easily remove them before they slide under the presser foot. Use fewer rather than more pins. They're just there to keep pieces lined up as you maneuver them on your sewing machine. Using too many pins can actually create puckered fabric in your seams.

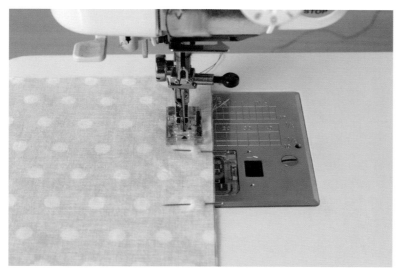

Pins should be perpendicular to seams.

PRESSING

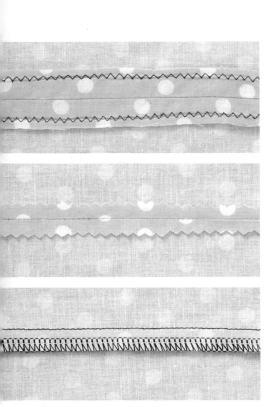

My students always love hearing how much pressing they'll do when sewing. Okay, maybe 1 in 100 loves ironing! Whatever your feelings about ironing, know that a garment must be properly pressed throughout the sewing process for it to look right when it's done.

Always start a project by ironing your fabric so it is nice and smooth before you start cutting your pattern.

If you pink or zigzag stitch your seams, press seams open when you encounter instructions to press your seams. Use your fingers to separate the seam allowance and then iron down the middle, along the seam. I always flip the garment and do a quick press on the right side, down the seam, to make sure I have not pressed in any puckers.

Serged seams can't be pressed open because the stitches are cast over the edge of the seam allowance. If you choose to serge your seams, press them to one side.

ROLLED HEM

This is a favorite use for my serger. Although some newer sewing machines use a special presser foot to create a rolled hem, it's really more of a narrow (⅛″ or less) hem. Follow the instructions in your serger manual to set up your machine for a rolled hem. Using Wooly Nylon or Bulky Nylon in the upper looper will provide heavier coverage of the fabric than standard polyester serger thread. I use a rolled hem on the bottom of skirts, ruffles, the edges of ruching, and sleeves. I've found that it's best to finish the edge with a rolled hem before sewing side seams to keep the serger from making a bubble over thicker fabric edges.

ROTARY CUTTING

The fastest, most efficient way to cut basic shapes, such as squares and rectangles, is with a rotary cutter and acrylic ruler. Hold down the ruler with the fingertips of your noncutting hand (kind of like fingertip pushups) to help keep it from slipping.

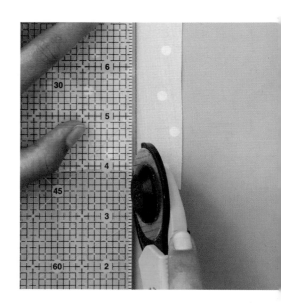

I also use my rotary cutter to cut around pattern pieces. I lay my ruler on top of straight edges to help me make fast, straight cuts. Around curves, I gently place my fingertips on the pattern and cut firmly and slowly around the curves. Sometimes, I use my scissors to cut especially tricky curves (like the Fly Facing on projects in the Pants chapter) or inverted points that my rotary cutter cannot reach. Always use great care—rotary cutters are razor sharp!

STRAIGHT STITCH

This is the most common stitch in your sewing arsenal, the one you'll use to construct probably every garment you ever make. Keep your stitch length at a short to medium length (I use 2.2) and sew along your pieces with the edge of your garment running along the seam allowance mark on your sewing machine. (The projects in this book most often use a ½″ seam allowance.)

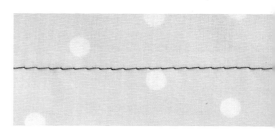

THREAD

Use good-quality thread in a color that matches the fabric. The examples in this book were sewn with contrasting thread for illustration purposes.

TOPSTITCHING

Topstitching is both functional and decorative. It helps maintain the integrity of your garment's shape and keeps seams flat on the inside. You can use a longer straight stitch (I set mine to 3.0) or a decorative stitch (zigzag or fancier). Stitches will be close to a garment's seam or edge. Within this book, topstitching is used around the bottom of the bodice where gathered panels attach, above tiers on skirts, and on the waistbands of pants.

: TIP

: When topstitching, I switch out my regular
: presser foot for a clear appliqué foot. It makes
: it easier to see seams.

Topstitch closely above seams after pressing seam allowances.

TRACING PATTERNS

The Bodice and Pants patterns from this book are printed on both sides of the pattern (pullout pages P1 and P2), with the intention of being traced before use. My choice is Easy Pattern (by Pellon), but you can use Pattern-Ease, Swedish tracing paper, clear landscape fabric from the garden center, or even lightweight interfacing. These provide you with a reusable pattern piece that's sturdier than tissue paper. It also lets you make the outfits from this book in multiple sizes without cutting into the nested patterns. I trace every pattern I sew and keep the traced pattern with the pattern envelope or book. Make sure you copy all the markings from the original pattern, including grainline, notches, number of pieces to cut, pattern name/number, and size.

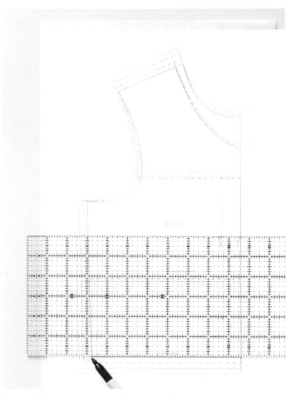

Tracing keeps your nested patterns intact.

UNDERSTITCHING

Understitching secures a lining or element (like a pocket) to a seam allowance so it automatically rolls to the inside of a garment. Press the lining over the seam allowance after sewing; then stitch close to the seam through the lining and seam allowance.

WAISTBANDS

Every project sewn for the bottom half of your child's body needs a waistband, whether you're making a casing for elastic or adding a set-on flat waistband.

Casing with Inserted Elastic

1. Fold over the edge of the waistband (the top edge of the skirt or pants) ¼″ to the wrong side of the fabric and press.

Fold top edge ¼″ to wrong side and press.

2. Fold over the edge another 1″, again to the wrong side of the fabric, and press again.

Fold over top edge another 1″ toward wrong side of fabric and press again.

3. With the garment wrong side out, stitch close to the bottom edge of the waistband all the way around, leaving a 1″ opening at the side seam or the center of the back. Be sure to backstitch at the beginning and end of your stitching.

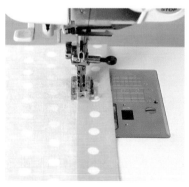

Stitch close to bottom edge of waistband casing.

4. Attach a bodkin or safety pin to an end of the elastic and guide it through the waistband casing.

5. When you get back to the opening, push the bodkin end through it.

6. Sew the elastic loop closed after you check one last time to make sure it's not twisted. You can either overlap the elastic ends about 1″ and use a zigzag stitch to secure them or abut the elastic ends and use a very wide zigzag stitch to connect the two without overlapping them. This latter option can take a little practice, but it creates a nice, flat waistband. For both methods, sew back and forth a couple of times to secure the elastic well.

TIP

I recommend securing the free end of the elastic to the garment with another safety pin to keep it from accidentally being pulled into the casing. Take care to keep the elastic flat as you feed it through so it doesn't end up twisted inside the casing.

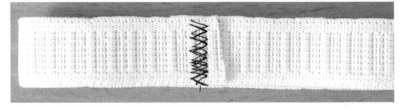

Overlapped elastic ends

Abutted elastic ends

7. After you connect the ends, slip the elastic through the gap in the casing and stitch the waistband gap closed. Take care not to stitch through the elastic. Turn your garment right side out. To prevent your waistband elastic from twisting, secure it to the side seams by stitching-in-the-ditch of the seamline. *Stitching-in-the-ditch* means sewing in the right side of the fabric in the seam where two pieces meet. The line of stitches virtually disappears into "the ditch."

Set-On Waistband

The Set-On Waistband is used on all of the Pants projects. It features a flat front and a casing in the back for buttonhole elastic to make an adjustable-fit waist. If desired, you can interface the exterior pieces of the Waistband with a midweight interfacing.

1. Match the short edges of the exterior Waistband Front to the exterior Waistband Back, right sides together. Pin and sew with a ½″ seam allowance. Press seam allowances open and clip the corners.

2. Match the short edges of the interior Waistband Front to the interior Waistband Back, right sides together. Pin. Starting at the top edge, sew ½″, leave a ⅞″ gap, and then sew ⅝″ to the bottom edge. Press seam allowances open and clip the corners.

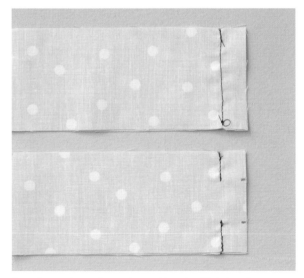

Sew short edges of exterior and interior Waistbands.

3. From the right side of the interior Waistband, topstitch along the seam allowances on both sides. Repeat this step on the other Waistband side seams.

Topstitch along seam allowance.

4. Match the top edges of the exterior Waistband and the interior Waistband, right sides together. Pin and sew using a ¼″ seam allowance. Press the seam allowance open.

5. Press the bottom edge of the interior Waistband ½″ toward the wrong side of the fabric.

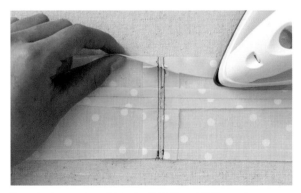

Press bottom edge of interior Waistband ½″ toward wrong side of fabric.

6. Match the right side of the exterior Waistband to the right side of the top edge of the Pants, starting at the side seams. The front edges of the Waistband will extend beyond the front opening of the Pants. Pin and sew using a ½″ seam allowance.

Match Waistband to top edge of Pants.

7. Press the Waistband up over the seam allowance.

8. Trim the front overlap to ½″.

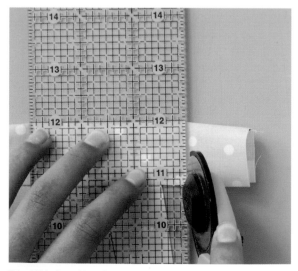

Trim Waistband overlap to ½″.

9. Fold the Waistband in half, right sides together. Pin the Waistband overlap and sew using a ½″ seam allowance. The line of stitches should be even with the Fly Facing / Fly Shield.

10. Clip the seam allowance, turn the Waistband right side out, and press.

Turn Waistband right side out and press.

11. Pin the open edge of the Waistband in place, matching the folded edge to the seam connecting the Waistband to the Pants.

12. From the right side of the Pants, topstitch the Waistband above the Pants seam, pivoting at the corners to stitch along the front edge opening and along the top edge of the Waistband.

13. Hand stitch ½″ buttons to the side seam allowance inside the Waistband, taking care not to stitch through to the outside of the Waistband.

14. Use a bodkin or safety pin to feed a piece of ¾″ buttonhole elastic through the back Waistband casing. Slip the buttonhole elastic over the buttons to fit.

ZIPPERS

I remember being intimidated by zippers, but a little bit of practice (and maybe a few zippers-gone-wrong) got me over the fear. Now I add them to all kinds of garments. The projects in this book use either an invisible zipper or a trouser zipper.

Invisible Zipper

Once you've mastered this technique, you'll be wishing you could add zippers to everything you sew. An invisible zipper foot—preferably one made for your sewing machine rather than a generic plastic version—is a must. Be sure to finish the seam allowances where you will insert the zipper first.

1. Remove the zipper from the package and lower the zipper head. Use an iron set to "synthetic" to press the teeth flat.

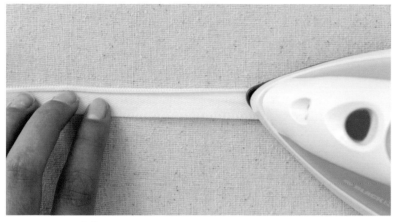

Press zipper teeth flat.

2. Match the right side of the left half of the zipper to the right side of the left back of the garment, ⅛″ from the center back edge.

TIP

Most invisible zippers are made with polyester fabric on the tape and nylon teeth. If you are not careful with the ironing, it is possible to actually melt the teeth of the zipper.

TIP

If inserting a zipper into a garment with the lining, push the lining out of the way while attaching the zipper. Afterward, press under the seam allowance on the lining and tack it to the zipper tape with a few hand stitches.

3. Measure from the center back edge to the right of the zipper teeth to ensure that you will have a seam allowance of ½″ at the center back. Adjust the zipper placement, if necessary.

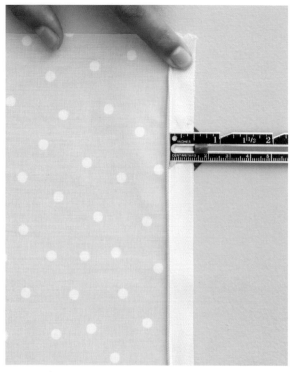

Measure from center back edge to right of zipper teeth.

4. Using your invisible zipper foot, sew the zipper close to the teeth, starting at the neckline. Stop above the zipper head.

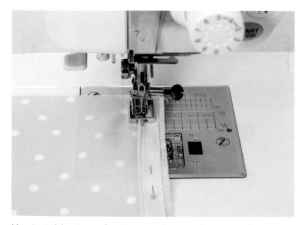

Use invisible zipper foot to sew close to zipper teeth.

5. Match the right side of the right half of the zipper to the right side of the right back of the garment, ⅛″ from the center back edge.

Match second half of zipper to opposite edge.

6. Check the zipper placement, as in Step 3.

7. With your invisible zipper foot, sew the zipper close to the teeth, starting at the neckline. Stop above the zipper head.

8. Close the zipper to check that it is inserted properly.

9. Flip the bottom of the zipper out of the way and match the center back seam below the zipper to the hem. Pin.

Pin center back below zipper and sew.

10. Starting at the bottom of the zipper stitching, sew the rest of the center back seam with a ½″ seam allowance.

11. Press the center back seam open.

TIP

I like to tack the bottom of the zipper to the seam allowance by hand with a few stitches.

Trouser Zipper

Do not be intimidated by the Trouser Zipper! Once you've sewn a couple of them, you'll be whipping up pants by the dozen. I recommend using a polyester zipper. However, once you get the hang of it, try using a more durable jeans zipper with metal teeth. Just make sure you don't try to sew through the zipper teeth!

1. Fuse interfacing to the wrong side of one Fly Shield and the wrong side of the right Pants Front Fly Facing, ½" beyond the trim line.

2. Trim the Fly Facing from the left Pants Front leg along the trim line on the sewing pattern.

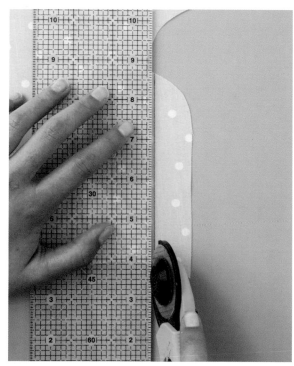

Trim Fly Facing from left Pants Front.

3. Match the Fly Shield pieces, right sides together. Sew along the curved edge using a ¼" seam allowance.

TIP

If you have the perfect zipper on hand but it's too long, use it anyway! Simply let the zipper tape extend above the top of the pants and trim the excess after sewing the first set-on waistband seam.

4. Turn the Fly Shield right side out and press.

5. Finish the raw edges of the Pants rise, including the Fly Facing, and the raw edge of the Fly Shield.

6. Mark ½" over from the edge of the Fly Facing.

7. Align the right edge of the zipper with the mark on the Fly Facing. Pin and sew in place, using a zipper foot to stitch close to the zipper teeth.

Pin and sew zipper to Fly Facing.

8. Align the right edge of the zipper with the overcast edge of the Fly Shield. Pin and sew in place, using a zipper foot to stitch close to the teeth.

Pin and sew zipper to Fly Shield.

9. Match the zipper edge of the Fly Shield to the trimmed section of the left Pants Front, right sides together. Sew in place, using a zipper foot to stitch on top of the line of stitches securing the zipper.

10. Press the seam toward the Pants Front and topstitch along the Pants, close to the seam with the Fly Shield.

Topstitch Pants close to seam with Fly Shield.

11. Press the Fly Facing to the wrong side of the Pants, making sure the center front seam is even with the seam allowance.

12. Pin the Fly Facing in place and sew ¼" from the edge on the wrong side of the Pants, starting at the top edge and ending just past the zipper teeth. Make sure the Fly Shield is away from the stitching.

Secure Fly Facing to Pants Front, ¼" from edge.

13. Press the Fly Shield into place.

14. From the right side of the Pants, set your sewing machine to a narrow zigzag stitch with a stitch length of 0. Stitch a bar tack ¼" above the Fly Facing stitching, securing the Fly Shield in place.

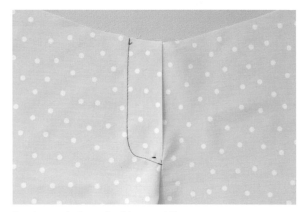

Sew bar tack through all layers of Fly.

About the Author

Photo by Jonah Rondon

After an award-winning print journalism career spanning nearly two decades, Mary Abreu left the newsroom to pursue her passion for sewing. Her first book, *Little Girls, Big Style*, was published in 2010. Mary also works as a seamstress with a boutique movie studio and has wardrobe department credits on two short films, including *The Candy Shop*, starring Doug Jones. She is an accomplished sewing instructor who teaches a wide range of classes near her metro Atlanta home. Mary enjoys attending pop culture conventions, where she is a regular presenter on the topics of pattern drafting and hacking, costuming for children, and historically influenced costuming. She lives with her family near Atlanta, Georgia. Visit her website: **confessionsofacraftaddict.com**.

FunStitch
✕ ✕ ✕ ✕ ✕ ✕ ✕ ✕ ✕ ✕
STUDIO

FunStitch Studio books are written and designed specifically with kids, tweens, and teens in mind!

"Every time I finish a project, **I get so excited**, because I feel like I can do **anything!**"
···· Annalise, age 12 ····

The text and projects are age appropriate and *nurture the love of handmade* in budding sewists, quilters, embroiderers, and fashion designers.

by Annabel Wrigley

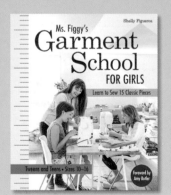

by Shelly Figueroa

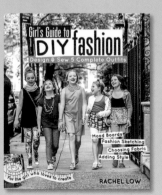

by Rachel Low

See the complete list of FunStitch Studio titles at ctpub.com/ funstitch-studio

an imprint of C&T Publishing